T0193420

Defining Truth

Definition Series - Volume 1

NANETTE T. FRIEND

authorHOUSE®

AuthorHouse™
1663 Liberty Drive
Bloomington, IN 47403
www.authorhouse.com
Phone: 1 (800) 839-8640

Published by AuthorHouse 11/05/2019

ISBN: 978-1-7283-2396-1 (sc)
ISBN: 978-1-7283-2395-4 (e)

Library of Congress Control Number: 2019912165

Print information available on the last page.

This book is printed on acid-free paper.

This is the true account of my perilous journey while incarcerated within a women's state prison. However, please understand that most all of the names and locations have been changed to protect the innocent and very sensitive nature of the stories portrayed within the series.

Scripture quotations marked NIV are taken from the Holy Bible, New International Version®. NIV®. Copyright © 1973, 1978, 1984 by International Bible Society. Used by permission of Zondervan. All rights reserved. [Biblica]

"As a prison ministry volunteer for several years, I eagerly read through Nanette's personal account of what led to her downfall and subsequent prison term. Her story drew me in, with its rare personal insight into the day-to-day grind of prison life. I was encouraged and blessed as I read how Ms. Friend learned to see God's loving and protective hand, in the darkest time of her life, giving her hope and courage. I look forward to reading the next book in her series!"

~ *Connie Cameron* Speaker and Author of ***Stories of Faith and Courage from Prison*** (AMG Publishers)

"In an age of seemingly negative cultural events, it is extremely refreshing to read of such an inspirational story of God's redemptive power to restore hope and purpose through a meaningful life. It is encouraging to see the promise of scripture come to life such as is found in Romans 8:28."
"28 And we know that in all things God works for the good of those who love him, who have been called according to his purpose."

~ *Scott Hayes* Chaplain | LC Jail Ministries

"As the Women's Chaplain of our local jail, I have had the privilege of serving in the jail ministry with the Author. Her heart is to reach the often shunned and rejected of society. Most inmates prefer not to ever step foot back in the Justice Center. However, as this book profoundly reveals, Nanette's heart is to give the glory to God! By reaching the down and out, her sweet spirit shines through this moving testimony. Her account of persistence and new found love of Jesus, will encourage the lost and the hopeless. A must read!"

~ *Patricia Collins* Women's Chaplain | LC Jail Ministries

Dedication

n: The act of dedicating; the state of being dedicated to (an event, project, time, etc.); a formal, printed inscription in a book, piece of music, etc. dedicating it to a person, cause, or the like.

In dedication and love to "Nana": As an author and journalist, you instilled within me a love for writing, as well as a heart for Jesus from the time I can barely remember. I know you would be proud that I have attempted to follow in your foot-steps.

To my Aunt Bev: From the time I was a small child, I have admired and respected your strong faith and Christian values. Always a houseful, yours was the place where all the kids from the neighborhood, as well as the church youth group, would hang out. It was within this loving, nurturing and safe home, you demonstrated the character, grace and love of Jesus to everyone you knew. When I was in prison you wrote to me, encouraging me, loving me and not judging me. When I came home, you hugged me tightly and gently whispered *"Just listen to Him, Nan. Just listen to what He tells you."* To this day, when I am experiencing worry or fear; or seeking an answer I desperately need, I can still hear your soft voice telling me *"Just listen to Him, Nan."*

To my very long-time friend, Gloria, for your early belief and encouragement of me: You told me many, many years ago that someday I should write a book of my "adventures." Years before my incarceration you saw something within me that I couldn't see myself. I still have in my possession the journal you gifted to me, and had written inside *"You can do it Nan. Write a best seller!"* I have never forgotten that. Thank you, my dear friend.

CONTENTS

n: The individual items or topics that are dealt with in a publication or document. The material, including text and images that constitutes a publication or document. The substantive or meaningful part: The meaning or significance of a literary or artistic work.

CONTENTS

Introduction

n: Formal personal presentation; preliminary part leading to the main part; something introduced.

"These are the things you are to do: Speak the truth to each other, and render true and sound judgment in your courts."
Zechariah 8:16

Defining . . .

n: The act of defining, distinct or clarify. Clear; the formal statement of the meaning or significance of the word, phrase, etc. The accuracy of sound or picture reproduction. Degree of clarity. Statement conveying fundamental character.

. . . Truth
n: the body of real things, events, and facts: the state of being the case: actual fact; often capitalized: a transcendent fundamental or spiritual reality: GOD; a judgment, proposition, or idea that is true or accepted as true; the body of true statements and propositions; the property (as of a statement) of being in accord with fact or reality; sincerity in action, character, and utterance.

By now you have no doubt realized each segment begins with a definition of the main theme for the chapter. In virtually every case, you will already know and understand the meaning of the word. However, my true desire is to draw attention to, and leave no uncertainty regarding the nature of each subject and what it will portray.

In each of our lives there lies within us our personality, our character, our values, and our true identity. It is what "defines" us. The choices we make, the things we cherish, or possibly "worship," the people or beliefs that influence us, and the hope we believe in, clearly makes us the person we are within. It is up to us to decide what we believe to be the "truth" about who we are, and what we believe to be actual or real events within our spirit.

From the time I was a very young, I have known in my heart I would someday write a book. I never knew exactly what I would write about, how I would accomplish it, or even why I should think I would have something so profound to say to the world. I only knew I would have a story to tell. A story that would be important. A story that would possibly, hopefully change a life; or at the very least, make an important difference to someone. To present something so significant, so essential to a persons' existence, they would finally say *"I get it!"* At long last, I now know what I am purposed to share.

Please understand this is *NOT* a "quick fix" book to boast of how you will find instant success, happiness or freedom from all of your struggles by submitting money, utilizing prayer cloths; or if you will only follow *"these 6 easy steps!"* I am certainly not going to tell you that you will come to realize you have an incredible universal or "spiritual" power within *yourself* (your **own** thoughts and power), and that if you will only *BELIEVE* in *yourself* enough, eventually the "universe" will give you everything you "deserve." What I am going to tell you is there is *REAL* and *GENUINE* hope, promise, and **truth** for each of you.

It is without question a huge responsibility to understand the words you speak or write are in fact truth, and nothing but the truth. I unmistakably acknowledge that someday I will stand before the Lord our God, and will answer for everything I will ever speak or write on His behalf. God's infinite grace will provide the time, the tools, the wisdom, the necessary provisions - as well as a time to heal, and a time to reflect. For the past several years I have asked "What do you want from me, God? What do you want me to do, to say?" His answer has always been ". . . *the truth. .*

. . just tell the truth."

And so it will be. This is the *true* account of my journey while incarcerated in a women's state prison. And although most of the names and locations have been changed to protect the innocent (and the guilty) and very sensitive nature of the stories portrayed within the series; let there be no mistake, however, that regardless of the stories revealed, or of the testimony portrayed within the pages of this manuscript - the only true definition I wish to convey without question is the understanding and defining clarity of the **Truth, Faith, Hope, Forgiveness, Grace, Love** and **Promise** of our Savior Jesus Christ. And how do we know who Jesus is? By reading and learning the truth from His word in the Bible – the *true* story of His life.

This first book will begin the story of my journey, my search, and my walk with God throughout the time I was incarcerated. Each subsequent book to follow will depict the previous mentioned (*Faith, Hope, Forgiveness, etc.*) true evidences of our gracious Lord at other significant times in my life.

"But the angel of the Lord by night opened the prison doors, and brought them forth, and said 'Go, stand and speak in the temple to the people all the words of this life."

Acts 5:19-20

CHAPTER 1

❧ *Anticipation* ❧

n: Realization in advance; expectation or hope; previous notion, impressions, intuition, or foreknowledge; an anxiety or knowledge of things before they exist or happen; foresight.

The First Day…of the Rest of My Life

The large, muscular dark-haired deputy assigned to transport me to the Women's State Penitentiary that brisk October morning, appeared to be surprised and bewildered upon first seeing me that particular day. I could sense the shifting of his eyes as he checked through the transference papers, looked up at me, and then back at the documents.

"Friend?"

"Yes, sir?" I replied, as he called my last name.

The touch of cold metal cuffs now shackled around my wrists and ankles, I was still clad in dress black slacks and heels, carefully matched to a polyester white blouse with small pearls layered delicately around the collar and down the front in a jacquard floral pattern. The ensemble was topped off with a black suit jacket. I had previously removed my pearl earrings upon leaving the courthouse, but still bore the delicate gold necklace bearing a small cross intertwined with silver.

Carrying a pair of off-brand, but sturdy tennis shoes in one hand, and a small paperback copy of the Bible in the other,

I had been informed these would be the only two items I would be permitted to take inside the prison with me.

Now seated in the sheriff's cruiser, I burrowed myself in the corner of the back seat. Thoughts resonated through my mind of my Mother's words, vocalizing to me the concern of my youngest sister, Abbie, a few days earlier. Fear and apprehension echoed back to me as my mother quietly repeated "She'll never make it there, Mom."

Peering through the rear-view mirror of the vehicle, the deputy made small talk. "You don't seem to be the kind of person who would be going to prison."

Sheepishly realizing this would be the last day I would be wearing make-up, jewelry and "street" clothes for a very long time, I couldn't respond to him; my head hung in shame. He continued his effort to make conversation, and inquired how much time I had been sentenced to serve. I softly answered "one year", suddenly gasping for breath; fighting back the tears I could feel welling up in my eyes.

I was sorely and profoundly terrified of what the next year would bring. The previous two years had been filled with agony, depression, confusion, fear, and suicidal attempts of what I had brought upon myself and my victims. I had finally come to realize that not only the members of the large six-state Association contracted with my company; but my children, family, friends and employees were also all victims of my crime. Every single one had loved and trusted me explicitly. Not one of them ever did anything to deserve the theft, lies, embarrassment nor shame I had conveyed upon them. I knew full well I deserved the punishment that had been bestowed upon me.

Traveling the highway of the nearly ninety-minute trip to the prison, I could only stare out the window with a deeper appreciation of the beautiful array of bright orange, red and gold fall colors adorning the trees along the highway. I knew it would be another full year before I could smell the fall air, or breathe the fresh scent of freedom again. I realized then how very much I had taken for granted the beauty of the earth God had given for me to enjoy.

A single mother of four children, always busy with work, home, school and sports activities, I never took the time to grasp or appreciate these daily gifts of magnificent splendor. I now gazed intently at the trees, trying to embed the exquisite perfection of God's masterpiece into my brain. I listened to the tranquil sound of the birds singing, attempting to capture the sound of peace and freedom in my head. I didn't want to forget what any of this looked, smelled or sounded like once I reached the prison.

Eventually turning into the long dirt and gravel driveway, and approaching the massive, tall, steely silver gates; I stared at the huge spiral stratum of barbed wire bound in six or seven layers along the top of the double rows of fencing. I gasped to myself *"Oh Nan, what in God's name have you done now?"* and wondered quietly *"What could you have possibly been thinking?"*

With a sickness deep within the pit of my stomach, and every part of my body aching with fear; I was only just beginning to fathom the realization of what I had become, and where I had taken my life. I had truly arrived at the end of the long and twisted road I had chosen. I could only surmise this was going to be the beginning of what I believed would be hell on earth for me. I could only comfort myself to a slighter degree by rationalizing *"Well, legally, they can't kill me."* Of course, *legally* was the operative word. I would soon come to realize many horrific stories regarding prison life were very true to form, and within the walls of the penitentiary is where all "fairness" and justice cease to have any power.

After the long and silent drive to the prison, the cruiser was escorted inside the entrance gates. No doubt sensing my anxiety and dreaded anticipation, the Deputy turned to me and said "Don't be afraid. Just stay to yourself and out of trouble and you'll be ok. Just do what they tell you and your time will go quickly."

As he escorted me through the double solid steel doors to the admissions area, I perceived what was possibly an afterthought and possible effort of empathy, he blurted out as he parted, "Good luck...you probably won't do all of your time." I was appreciative of his compassion to me, a criminal who didn't deserve to hear those words. I jumped at the immense sound of the final door slamming behind me, the automatic locks grinding against the steel, and the overwhelming fear of knowing I was now firmly locked within these walls.

The "admissions" officer who met us at the front corridor led me into a small enclosed room of concrete walls, painted a dull gray with no windows, and only a small wooden bench against the wall. The female Corrections Officer ("CO") instructed me to wait on the bench until she came back with a small white towel, plastic squeeze bottle with some form of clear green liquid, and an empty shipping box. Directing me around the corner to the cold, drab shower area; I was ordered to disrobe completely, and place all of my clothing, heels and jewelry in the box. I was permitted to keep my watch upon having my new identity of an assigned "inmate number" securely engraved on the back.

I could once again feel the sickness growing within my stomach; this time due to the excruciating humiliation of having my entire body and head now completely exposed, and searched for lice. Opening my mouth to have the "CO" run her white latex gloved fingers along my teeth and gums, I was mortified as she further ordered me to stick out my tongue, squat and cough hard three times in order to determine if I was concealing drugs or other contraband within the "cavities" of my body. Ordered to step into the icy, dark shower stall devoid of any curtain to provide a semblance of privacy; I quivered as I poured the cold, watered-down lice shampoo onto my head. "Scrub your hair, rinse and step out," the officer commanded.

The anticipation and dread of what could happen next was unbearable. Or could this get any worse? My throat incredibly dry, I could barely breathe as the weight of my sin seemed to crush my lungs and heart. I truly longed to be dead. In my mind, death at this point would possibly be best for everyone anyhow, as I thought of the horrific pain and humiliation I had brought upon my victim and my family. I wanted to scream in disgust and degradation as the full body search continued. What on God's earth had I become to bring me to this point in my life?

My long dark hair still damp, and now matted into a large heap of tangles, I wrapped the small towel around my shivering body. A clear plastic bag marked with a large "L" (large size), containing a pair of neatly folded underwear, socks, bra and state-issued jumpsuit, were placed upon the bench. "Get dressed and meet me in the room next door for intake," the CO directed. I dried off and wrapped the towel around my head. The last article of clothing I pulled from the bag consisted of an oversized one-piece, washed out, army-green jumpsuit with obvious stains and holes. I quickly stepped into the outfit, and pulled the zipper up.

After heaps of paperwork, and eventually directed to sit in the front row of a long line of cold, metal folding chairs in the main foyer of the admissions building, I held tightly onto the allotted bedroll and white netted garment bag issued to me. Filled with an extra jumpsuit, two pair each of new state-issued white socks, non-underwire bras, underwear and towels, a small plastic cup, cheap toothbrush, and pocket-size black hair comb; this now encompassed my entire worldly possessions for the next 12 months.

Waiting with about 30 other "newbies" who *rode in* that day, "intake" procedure continued for what seemed to be countless hours. Not aware of what time it might be, we sat silently, not permitted to speak with each other. Called in one by one for "mug" shots, fingerprinting, blood draws, urine (drug) tests, and a complete pelvic and internal physical examination by a doctor; we continued to wait for further instructions, as well as unit and bed assignments. On several occasions throughout the process, groups of inmates were ushered through the intake area, laughing and jeering at us, shouting obscenities and "picking" out their future "mates."

"Hey pretty girl! What's your name?" I didn't look up. I didn't know, but didn't want to know who they were talking to.

I don't remember eating that afternoon, but I am sure we must have been offered food at some point. Still reeling from the sickness in my stomach from the stress, fear, and anticipation of what was yet to come, I couldn't imagine I could have possibly held anything down anyhow. Terror of the unknown continued to fill my mind and body. *"Please God, Please protect me,"* I whispered to myself. I imagined that possibly other newbies were likely whispering the same prayer, regardless of their religious devotion.

Eventually we were assigned to our bunks. Allocated a top bunk with no ladder, or from my 5' 2" standpoint, any conceivable way to climb onto the bed, I was certain this was a mistake. In my early forties and overweight by at least 40 pounds, I was sure there were plenty of young, skinny girls who could easily make that climb to the top bunk. Making my way back across the corridor to request a bottom bed, I suddenly heard whistles screeching, and shouting from the CO's desk, *"Count Time! On your bunk!"*

A look of terror and confusion in my eyes, my lower bunkmate yelled "You better get on that bunk *now*!"

I cried out "I can't! How am I going to get up there?"

She hurriedly pulled out her metal lockbox from underneath the lower bunk and snapped "Step on this and then on the end of the bed. Hurry up!" In a panic, I climbed as fast I could, slamming my shin on the metal railings of the bed.

"Now sit at the end and don't talk!" she quietly ordered. I hurriedly glanced around the large dorm to see how everyone else was positioned to make certain I wasn't caught "out of place."

Attempting to recall the "rules" from the manual given to us previously that day, I knew that being caught "out of place" was an automatic "ticket" and an appearance before the Sergeant. Unless otherwise granted permission at certain times of the day for meals, showers, library, classes, work assignments, or time allotted in the "yard", your designated bunk, and 24 inches on any side of the perimeter of your bunk, was the only place you were permitted to be. Four times throughout the day and night, *count time* was imposed, and we were required to be either sitting *Indian style,* or standing at attention at the end of our bunk facing the long corridor of beds.

As the night shift CO began the long, slow walk down each side of the walkway, she eventually made her way to my assigned area and stopped. Detecting a new face, she glanced up at me with a puzzled look. "Name?" she demanded.

"Nanette Friend," I swallowed hard.

"Number?" she shouted. In my fear, I hesitated. I looked confused. "Number!" she barked again.

Gulping with dread, I asked "The number they gave me today?"

As she peered down at her clipboard, she slowly raised her eyes and glared at me over the top of her glasses with an obvious look of disgust and impatience; then slowly drew out a very frustrated "Yeess!"

I attempted to read upside down the badge now attached to the front of my jumpsuit, and stuttered "46134".

"Memorize it!" she snapped back. Not even twelve hours, and already I was being scolded.

Count time now completed, the chatter of over three hundred women filled the huge open dorm like birds in a cage. I leaned over the side of the bunk and told the woman beneath me "Thanks."

"For what?" she answered.

"For helping me get up here." I offered.

"You better learn them rules real quick, 'cause it don't matter 'round here. They don't care if you don't know. You better be on that bed!" she warned.

"Ok" I stammered.

"Your last name is Friend?" she asked.

I welcomed the opportunity to talk a little. "Yes".

"For real? That's your name?" she chuckled.

"Yeah, for real. What's your name?" I inquired.

"Nothin' great. Baker." she responded. The conversation continued for a short while as she explained no one uses their first name here, as well as other various rules, times to eat, directions to the bathrooms, and a lot of "need to know" information. Mattie, as I soon learned her first name to be, offered stern warnings regarding staying out of trouble and away from certain hard-core trouble-makers in the dorm. I was appreciative of any advice she could offer.

Still feeling the numbness and tingling of my bruised shin, I leaned over the top of the bunk and said "I'm going to tell them I need a bottom bunk. I'm too old to be climbing up on this bed without a ladder."

"Girl, you forget where you are! You ain't going to tell them nothing'. You the prisoner! You lookin' for trouble or somethin'?" Mattie gasped.

"No" I whispered.

"Well, unless you sick, pregnant or disabled, you don't get a bottom bunk!"

Probably only in her mid-to-upper twenties, I couldn't help but wonder how Mattie got a bottom bunk. She was a little on the chunky side, but pretty healthy looking to me. I was afraid to ask her if she was pregnant. A young white girl with long soft, but mousy brown hair, I was sure this was not Mattie's first time in a jail or prison. She was very knowledgeable about a lot of the do's and don'ts, and seemed to be pretty *street smart*. I was thankful God had sent Mattie to help me in this place.

I continued to sit on the edge of my bunk for a short while, taking in what was to become my home for the next several weeks. Mattie introduced me to some of those around us, and we continued with small talk.

"So, what was your crime Friend? Forget to go to church or somethin'?" an inmate smirked at me.

"Yea, I guess I did. Something like that," I quickly offered. I knew I hadn't been to church in years. But I offered her no other explanation.

Grateful I was placed only three beds from the CO's desk, I felt somewhat comforted I hadn't been assigned near the back where no one could see what was going on. I noticed a large round black and white clock above the CO's desk. It was almost 8:00pm. I finally felt some form of association with the outside world as I realized what time it was.

Eventually, I lay down on my bunk. I tried to calm down and just keep to myself. The huge "football stadium" lights attached directly above our bunks were merciless as they beamed a powerful and overwhelming bright light. As the foul-mouthed, disrespectful, fighting, screaming, and often threatening language of many of the women continued, I knew this was going to be a long, sleepless night. I quickly surmised this was indeed the *devil's playground.*

I knew that many of the women being transferred in were still experiencing withdrawal symptoms from drug usage, and the constant, all-night screaming and cursing would only continue with each new group of inmates. Covering my face with the heavy, coarse "army" blanket I was allotted, I tried to tune out the loud noise and intense lights; but the brilliant illumination and obnoxious noise continued well into the night.

A thousand thoughts swirled through my head as I thought about this day. I wondered where my youngest daughter, Jennifer, was. Sixteen years old and the last one of my children left at home, did she stay at the house with my boyfriend, Don, so she could still go to school; or did she go to my parents' house that night? Was she able to sleep? Was she safe? Had she been able to eat anything? Did she hate me terribly for leaving her? I didn't blame her, for I hated myself. Did she even go to school that day? What kind of horrible situations did she face that day with her friends and teachers because she was embarrassed and humiliated by her mother? I couldn't even imagine what I must be putting her through. I left a book on her pillow that morning entitled *"Prayers on my Pillow"*, hoping she might find some kind of solace; or possible forgiveness of me.

How were my other children, my family, and Don all coping with this whole situation, I solemnly wondered to myself. I had left them all to face the disturbing and shocking questions about where I was, and how on earth this could have happened? Other than the small, initial article under *Court News* in the local newspaper almost two years earlier, very few people had even asked any of my children or family about anything. What would they say now?

Filled with anxiety, fear, and anticipation of what was to become of me, I determined I was already "out of place." This was not where I belonged. As I slowly drifted in and out of a brief, restless sleep from sheer mental exhaustion, I could only speculate of what was to come in the months ahead. This was *not* something I had ever dreamed would happen to me. This was without question a far cry, and different form of any anticipation or expectation of anything I could have ever imagined.

"20 Then Jacob made a vow, saying, "If God will be with me and will watch over me on this journey I am taking. . ."

Genesis 28:20

CHAPTER 2

❧ *Creation* ❧

n: The act of creating; especially the act of bringing the world into ordered existence; the act of making, inventing, or producing: as something that is shaped, formed, coined, fashioned, produced, as an original work of art.

"¹ In the beginning . . . ² God created the heavens and the earth. . . . " ²⁶ Then God said, "Let us make mankind in our image, in our likeness . . . ²⁷ So God created mankind in his own image, in the image of God he created them; male and female he created them. . ."

Genesis 1:1,2 and 26-27

God created me . . . in His own image. How could that possibly be true? To know God is to know that He *is* Love, He *is* Pure, He *is* Perfection, and He *is* Truth. To imagine that God would create someone who would eventually become the deceitful and corrupt person I had unmistakably become, was inconceivable to me.

The second day . . .

The glaring lights and offensive noise of the previous night had barely subsided when the loud repetitive sound of "switching" the stadium lights back up at 4:00am, awoke me from a very disturbed and restless night. Immediately, literally hundreds of women began to scramble off their bunks, awkwardly and hastily making their way to the bathroom in order to secure a spot at one of only 20 small white sinks, or 24 open-stall, dirty toilets. I slowly made my way to the open hall, waited in line for several moments, and noticed how quickly everyone scrubbed their face, combed through their hair, or sneaked to rinse out soiled underwear or socks in the sink when the CO wasn't watching. Other inmates sneered and cursed at those washing out dirty laundry. "Uuuooo! That is nasty! Don't wash your skanky drawers in *MY* sink, you b****!"

It was only then that I realized I had forgotten to bring the roll of toilet paper that had been provided to me. Not knowing anyone, and certainly not about to ask to borrow any, I made my way back to my bunk. I knew I would have to take my place at the end of the long line again, and be rushed to finish washing up and brushing my teeth. I felt so dirty, and showers would not be permitted until the assigned day for our dorm, once every three days.

There was also the pressure of knowing that only thirty minutes were allotted to get dressed and ready for the day; and the next half-hour assigned to make beds, and sweep and mop the floor in your 24-inch perimeter. There were noticeable, black scuff marks on the floors around my bunk. On my hands and knees trying to scrape them off, Mattie offered "Use your soap bar. That stuff will take anything off!"

Issued inside the basic package of personal items, was a single aqua blue bar of lye soap made by the women on the prison grounds. I remembered my Grandma Braxton using lye soap for cleaning when I was young; and the strong warnings she cautioned not to touch the soap because lye was a strong, caustic chemical that could eat right through your skin. Grandma had further instructed me to wash my hands thoroughly with hot water and rinse with a little vinegar. I had concluded using lye soap was pretty much pointless if you had to rinse it off immediately because it would burn your skin. But those scuff marks came right up, and that floor was looking pretty spotless.

"Count!" the CO shrieked throughout the dorm. It was 5:00am, and we were ordered to stand at the end of our bunk, ready for inspection. The CO made her way down each side of the long rows of bunks, shouting out each name, inspecting every area, and barking orders to those who had not made their bed, or dressed properly.

Across the aisle from me was an older black woman, most probably in her fifties or even sixties. She had dark wiry, unkempt hair that looked like it had been tied in knots; and was wearing shiny black patent leather shoes that looked so out of place with her tattered and worn dark-green jumpsuit. She had just come in the previous day with my group, and had lain in her bed the entire time, crying and moaning. The other women had taunted her throughout the night, yelling at her to shut-up and quit whining. I could only imagine that she was suffering from some form of withdrawal.

"What's your name?" the CO inquired. No response from the woman.

"What is your name?" the CO demanded again.

"Bertie" the old woman quietly answered as she rolled over in her bed and adjusted the oversized black framed glasses she was wearing.

"What's wrong with you that you can't get up and stand at the end of your bed?" the CO snapped. The woman was ordered to her feet, and then promptly scolded for her insubordination.

Inspections continued for possible contraband, missing or stolen items, and any disturbances reported throughout the night. I stood at attention while some were ordered to the Sergeant's office, and others were issued warnings.

"When you are dismissed from inspection, you will remain on your bunk until mail and breakfast call." A slight pause, and then "Dismissed!" the CO barked.

I knew there would be no mail for me yet. I would initially be issued three each of paper, envelopes and pencils so I could contact my family with the address and required information in order to write to me. Instructions, among other stipulations, would be to include my inmate number on the outside of the envelope, or the mail would be returned without question. In addition, family could only send in three sheets of paper and/or pre-stamped envelopes, pictures, copies of poems, articles, etc. Money Orders only would be accepted that must include your name and state number, in order to place money on your "books". However, no books, magazines, posters, large pads of paper, writing or art materials (color pencils), etc., would be permitted to be mailed in.

I wanted to ask Don to please send money in order that I could purchase additional writing paper, envelopes, a pen, and personal items like shampoo and deodorant. But for right now, I could only bide my time. Not permitted to make any phone calls for thirty days, I felt completely isolated and cut-off from everyone.

Ordered by rows to the cafeteria for breakfast, a large handwritten sign at the entrance informed us there was no butter, milk or salt available that day. The sign further instructed to take only one cup of juice or water. Several CO's roamed the corridors and food service area, constantly shouting various commands. "There will be NO talking! Do not get out of line, or you will be removed from the line with NO breakfast. Do NOT give or trade food with others, or keep any food to take back with you. Do NOT leave the food service area until you are dismissed, and NO shoving, punching or hitting." *Dang.* I was beginning to feel fearful just to eat meals.

The food was bearable, but bland and tasteless. I could barely choke down the overcooked and unsavory scrambled eggs, or dry toast on my tray. The "juice" was a bittersweet concoction of watered-down orange powered mix. Cautious not to speak a word, I could only stare at my plate and chew my food as quickly and quietly as possible. I was growing more nervous as there were several women causing a disturbance, and the CO ordered them to leave the area. An inmate sitting directly across from me asked if I was going to eat my toast.

"Come on, they don't feed you enough in here. I'm hungry!" Not looking up or acknowledging her, and knowing I wasn't about to give it to her, I hurriedly shoved it in my mouth and prayed for her to be quiet. I didn't want to get reprimanded or sent out of the cafeteria.

"Please God . . . please make her shut-up! I don't need any trouble in here!"

After breakfast, I wandered back to my area, and attempted to make my way back up on the top bunk again. I was getting a little better about getting on the bed, but a chore for me none-the-less. To this day I bear a scar on my left shin from the bruises I received from consistently striking my legs on the metal rails.

The lights now turned back to a low dim, and with only three or four hours of rest, most everyone went back to their bunks to sleep. Some went out into the yard for ten minutes to smoke or just get some fresh air. From my top bunk view I could see it was still very dark outside.

"We can go out in the yard later. It's too damn cold to go out there this early!" Mattie informed me.

I was relieved to be able to just lie on the bed for a while with some form of quiet time. I rolled up the heavy, dark blue hooded, state-issued coat we had been provided, and placed it under my head for a pillow. I tried to fall back to sleep, but my mind continued to wander.

Reflection . . .

It was Wednesday morning. Everyone at home would be on their way to school or work. I wondered how they were doing, and what they must be going through or thinking right now. I had failed everyone miserably. I was terribly worried about all my children; but more than anything I agonized the most about Jennifer, my youngest. During the two years since I had turned myself in, there were months and months of preliminary investigation, fact-finding and many things to be determined as this was my first and only criminal offence. Because I was initially told there was a very good possibility I would never serve any time, I hadn't told Jen anything at all until the previous week-end.

Children of God . . .

"When Jesus saw this, he was indignant. He said to them, "Let the little children come to me, and do not hinder them, for the kingdom of God belongs to such as these."

Mark 10:14

A beautiful girl voted to be Homecoming queen two years in a row, and on every court throughout her high school years, Jen was admired and well-liked. A cheerleader and hard worker at her after-school job, she had no idea what I had done, what was about to happen, or that I would be leaving her for an entire year. I thought I was protecting her by not telling her;

and now she had to face everything all by herself. My three oldest children were aware of the situation, and although very worried and upset, they were all married and lived in their own homes. I guess I felt they could somehow depend, and lean on each other.

Jen and I lived together in a small apartment, along with my boyfriend, Don. Staying with her father right now was not an option that she wanted to consider. He had not really been around since he left us when she was only eighteen-months old, and she didn't feel comfortable staying with him and his new wife right now. They also lived in another town. Suffering enough humiliation and pain, Jen pleaded with me that she wanted to stay home, be able to continue to go to her own school, and be with her friends right now. That was completely understandable.

I also knew she didn't want to stay with my parents who were very strict and demanding. My dad could be harsh and hurtful, and I had my own genuine concerns for not feeling comfortable about her living with them. Jen begged me to please allow her to stay home so she could stay in her own room and continue with her normal routine. However, Don insisted he didn't want her to stay there with him. He said he was afraid of what others would think, or possibly accuse him of. He insisted "It just isn't right! And you can't expect me to take care of her. She has a mind of her own and does as she pleases! I don't want that responsibility!"

I understood his reasoning; I really did. But I also understood that everyone was just expecting Jen to up and change her whole life when she was already going through so much. I was devastated none-the-less that Don wasn't willing to help me with this. We had been together almost four years, and I always thought he cared for Jen and would be more than willing to allow her to stay in our home with him. I had signed all the papers so that he would have temporary legal guardianship of her, and could cash the child support checks - but he was fighting it all the way. He insisted she would have to stay with my parents. After I said my good-byes and he dropped me off at court that morning, I didn't know where my daughter was.

Sighing with worry, I turned over on my side and tried to force myself to sleep a little. I was filled with disgust of myself that I had hurt so many, and now had no idea or control about how to repair the damage I had created. My life as I knew it before was now over. I could never go back. I could never undo all the ugly lies, theft and deception. I didn't know how to "fix" it anymore.

As tired and emotionally drained as I was, I still couldn't sleep. I thought about my family life while growing up. What had this young Catholic girl from a small collegiate town in the Midwest done to reach this dreadful point?

My parents were stern in the upbringing of their children, and expected us to be obedient, truthful and respectful in every way. The second oldest of eight children, and the oldest daughter, I was required to help with many of the household chores and care of my younger siblings. There was never a question that I should study hard, get good grades or go to church every Sunday. Not that I disagreed with those values, but life in the Braxton family was not what the outside world perceived it to be.

The oldest of the Braxton children, Mark was exactly one year older than me to the very day. Two years after me, Chuck was born, and then each year, one right after the other was Danny, Beffie, Abbie, and PJ. However, it would be another ten years before baby brother Mitchell would make himself known to the world. We laughed, played, teased, and taunted each other; but most always with the love and concern that siblings have for each other. Mom was a stay-at-home mother, and worked from morning to night taking care of the household and children.

Of the very strong mindset that the man was most certainly the "authority" within the household; without doubt my father's words were not to be questioned, and were the ultimate and authoritative truth and answer to everything. Required to respond with the respectful response of "yes sir" or "no sir" from the time we were able to speak, I am certain I believed that if my father had said it would snow on a hot July afternoon, I would have run to the window to wait for the arrival of the snowfall!

Daddy firmly believed a women's responsibility was to stay home, have babies, wash and iron clothes, cook, clean and tend the garden. From the time I was about 14-years old, I had come to realize becoming married would be my only "fate" in life; as we lived under the authority of a father who believed that girls absolutely did not pursue formal education, or ever consider a career in the work field. I had often dreamt of the day I would be able to go to college, but that would not be something I could ever believe would come true for me. College was something that would strictly be reserved for the five boys in the family to consider at best. However, a hard-working blue-collar man all of his life, eventually promoted to management, and then eventually the owner of his own business, our father did not believe anyone required advanced education to be successful.

Regardless, Dad worked two jobs for as long as I could remember to support our ever-growing family. He was gone most of the week, and often times when we did see him, most usually only on Sundays; he was tired, short-tempered and agitated. Over time he began drinking more and more with his friends after work at his 2nd shift job, and would then become verbally and sometimes physically abusive toward us; but most especially to our mother. I began to withdraw more and more from his presence, and often hoped he would never come home at all.

Make Love, Not War

A term once used to describe consumer buying habits and socially accepted behaviors for the majority of a population, toward the late 1960's the term "popular culture" was shortened to "pop culture" to describe the now rebellious habits and lifestyle of the youngest consumers. Assuming that pop culture was also the time when the hard-rock music world, Woodstock, free-flowing marijuana and "free love" of the 1960's and 70's hit; I was most definitely around for that.

I was fifteen the summer of 1970 when the entire family of seven children (youngest brother Mitchell not born yet), maternal grandparents Nana and Papa, and the family dog packed into a huge recreational vehicle, and traveled to the west coast and open space of the country. Once a carpenter by trade, Papa had built a large trailer to carry all of the luggage, boxes of canned food, 4 bicycles, a motorbike, his wheelchair, a large cage for Baron (our dog), and many other "need to have" supplies for our six-week vacation. As we made our way through several states, including Texas, New Mexico and Nevada, I was in awe of a world I had never known before.

Traveling the coastline of California, however, I watched in total wonderment of the younger generation playing on the beaches of San Diego; and strolling the streets of Los Angeles and San Francisco in their tie-dye shirts, big floppy hats, wire-rimmed sunglasses and bell-bottom blue jeans. Not permitted to date, let alone *think* about free love and drugs, I soon determined that my plan would be to graduate high school, immediately get married to my (secret) boyfriend, and finally be free of my parent's rigid rules. I longed for the freedom of the Hippies of my up-coming generation... traveling the country in Volkswagen buses, peace signs, and smoking "pot". I understood this to be a new and liberating way of life, and I wanted to be on board. I desperately wished to flee my rigid and somewhat dysfunctional home life.

"Red"...

Call was made to go outside to the "yard". It was almost 9:00am by now. I decided to get out even if only for a few moments. Pulling the large coat up over my arms and zipping it closed, I walked out into the frosty morning. Feeling the brisk frigid air stinging my cheeks, I huddled up against the building to break the wind. A woman with long red hair came and stood next to me. I recognized her as one of the inmates who had processed in with me. She told me her name, but explained everyone called her "Red."

A short stocky, true red-head with freckles, blue eyes and long wavy hair sculptured into braids, she resembled an innocent farm girl somewhere in her late twenties. We talked for the length of the yard break, sharing our fear as this was the first time in prison for both of us; our uncertainties about a lot of the other women, and what we were *in* (serving time) for. Red had been charged with assault with a deadly weapon as she had stabbed her boyfriend with a screwdriver.

"What? How the heck did that happen?" I asked, and then began to wonder if I should even be talking to this crazy woman.

"We were drinking heavy one night, like we usually do, but then got into a big fight. Butch started hitting me and chased me outside. I was running to get away from him, but he got a hold of me and started beating me with his fist. I got away and ran back up on the porch and grabbed a screwdriver. I told him to stay away from me, but he lunged at me, and I let him have it. I stabbed him right in his good leg. I warned him to stay away!"

Fascinated by her story, I listened more as she explained how she had called the Sherriff, and that Butch then got into a fight with the deputy.

"The cop was trying to make him stop yelling and fighting, and he had him down on the ground. Butch was wrestlin' around and then the cop pulled his leg off!"

"What? He pulled his leg off? What do you mean?" I asked in disbelief.

"Butch has a wooden leg, and that cop was trying to hold him down. But when Butch got up to run, the cop pulled his leg right off. You should have seen the look on his face!"

We both laughed out loud. It felt so good to finally be able to laugh at something.

"13For you created my inmost being; you knit me together in my mother's womb. 14 I praise you because I am fearfully and wonderfully made; your works are wonderful; I know that full well. 15My frame was not hidden from you when I was made in the secret place, when I was woven together in the depths of the earth. 16Your eyes saw my unformed body; all the days ordained for me were written in your book before one of them came to be."

Psalm 139:13-16

CHAPTER 3

❧ *Condition* ❧

n: A particular mode of existing state of a person or thing; situation with respect to circumstances; state of health, fit or requisite state; social position; restricting, limiting, or modifying circumstances, provision, or stipulation to make or establish a conditional response.

The next several days were a myriad of continued fear, confusion and commotion. Assigned to the "Admissions" building for approximately 30 days, everyone came through this area when first transported inside the prison. Each new inmate would be medically and mentally evaluated, receive their classified "status" (low, medium or high risk) and state-issued inmate number; as well as appointed jobs and assigned housing quarters within the general "population" of the reformatory.

The intake area branched off into four separate wings. Two of the units housed approximately 300 women each. Two very long stone walls, roughly fifty-yards in length and 8-feet high, ran through the center of the room; with bunk beds placed head to head on each side of the partition. From the top bunk there was only about 12 inches of privacy from the person on the other side of the wall. Eventually I came to realize I actually preferred the upper bunk as I had a good view of the entire room, as well as to be able to see out of the windows placed around the perimeter of the room, approximately 7-8 feet from the floor. In addition, I felt much safer and not so isolated from the protection of the guards. A lot of harassment, stealing, bullying and other acts of badgering seemed to be going on in the bottom bunks where the women were sheltered from security.

The third branch was a "boot camp" for those who qualified for an intense "drug-rehab" program. For approximately 30 women at a time, this was a one-time only opportunity to go through a 12-week course; and if able to successfully graduate, the candidate would not be required to serve the remainder of their sentence. For admission and eligibility to the camp, it was required to have an original sentence of only two years or less for a drug charge; no charges of violence, child endangerment or drug activity within any school area, as well as a multitude of other stipulations. Isolated from the rest of the population, these women neither ate, showered, nor were permitted outside in the yard at the same time as the other inmates. Nor were they able to speak to, or acknowledge others in any way. Prisoners were encouraged, and would often taunt, mock and catcall these women just trying to get them to break, laugh, or lose their composure, which would be grounds for immediate dismissal from the program.

Required to iron their two-piece gray "uniforms" to be without spot or wrinkle, beds to be made with military crispness, and hair to be combed back and braided at all times, these "boot camp" ladies were to *toe the mark* in every way. I would sometimes watch from the windows as these "soldiers" would perform countless calisthenics, run for hours, and receive very few breaks when they were permitted to rest in the grass from sheer exhaustion.

Early one morning as I looked on, the ladies were ordered to complete 100 push-ups in the hall-way of the building. One of the women became physically ill, throwing up all over the newly shined waxed floor. The sergeant in command stopped in front of her, screaming as loud as she could, "Pick yourself up and count it out! Who told you, you could be sick?! Did I give you permission to puke on my floor? Now start counting or you're outta here!"

I watched in total disbelief as the young girl raised herself up, began to continue with the push-ups and yell out every count, each time her nose only inches from the vomit she had just dispelled. I was in awe that she didn't even grimace or give any indication that she was sickened by all of this. When morning exercises were completed, she was instructed to scrub and wax the floor again. I knew it had to take great determination, perseverance, and strength of character to continue with and complete this grueling program.

The fourth branch housed all of the offices, classrooms, processing areas (pictures, fingerprinting, badges, etc.), kitchen and library. In the center of the module where each of the areas branched off of, was the large circular atrium where the CO's main desks were situated. Behind the desks were closets filled with cleaning supplies, brooms and mops of which were used each day to clean the building.

Every inmate processed in was integrated with everyone else within the Admissions area, regardless of the crime. Mixed in with women who had not paid child support, charged with drug trafficking, arson, robbery or possibly aggravated theft, I slept in a bunk next to a woman convicted of multiple murders.

In a state of disbelief, I listened as many of the women spoke of their mothers, aunts, sisters, neighbors and even daughters who were serving time with them. Others spoke of their children on the outside they had not seen for months or even years, as these women had been in and out of the "system" so many times. Some didn't even know where their children were. Many chuckled about how they just kept coming back through the *revolving door*. I could only think to myself "*What did you not figure out the first time that you keep coming back to someplace like this?"*

Many formed their own "families" within the prison walls; having a "Dad" (head of the family), Mom, aunts, sisters and brothers, for those who preferred to be of the masculine gender. You didn't dare cross the line of those within the "family", and could only be *invited* in to be a member of the household. I realized this had become a way of life for many of the women, and this truly *was* their only family. But this was not anything I ever hoped to understand or be a part of. I just wanted to go home and be with my own family of children and grandchildren.

I was beginning to understand more and more that this situation had become yet one more chapter of the same inexplicable situation in my life, playing itself out over and over again. After several years of pain, abuse, shame and brokenness from the time I was a child, the condition of my life had grown dismal and grim. The condition of my soul was meaningless. The condition of my mind was empty and bitter. The condition of my heart was hopeless. I had given up on any thought that God had ever loved me. I still believed He existed - just not for me.

Condition . . . of my soul

When Jesus saw him lying there and learned that he had been in this condition for a long time, he asked him, "Do you want to get well?"

John 5:6

The man lying by the pool had been crippled and an invalid for 38 years. He explained to Jesus that he had no one to help him. Jesus then commanded him

8... "Get up! Pick up your mat and walk." 9 At once the man was cured; he picked up his mat and walked".

12 So they asked him, "Who is this fellow who told you to pick it up and walk?" 13 The man who was healed had no idea who it was, for Jesus had slipped away into the crowd that was there."

John 5:8-9 &12-13

I always knew who Jesus was. I well remember my grandmothers reading many Bible stories, and teaching me several songs that children sing in Sunday school class. By the age of three, I had memorized *"Jesus Loves Me This I Know..."* and *"He's Got the Whole World in His Hands"*. My favorite, however, was to play the hand game, "Here's the church, here's the steeple, open the doors and out come the people!" as I would giggle and wiggle my pudgy little fingers up in the air.

Mom always made certain that without fail, every one of us attended Mass each Sunday, as well as catechism classes on Saturday morning. It was all so confusing to me, however. Before the inception of Vatican II Council in 1965, the entire Mass was spoken in Latin. I didn't have a clue what anyone was saying. Mom was adamant that we should partake of the Holy Sacraments, but often times I didn't even comprehend most of it. Unmistakably, I sensed the reverence and respect for the church, yet everything just seemed so rigid and stern. Not at all like the love of the Jesus my grandmothers had told me about. I had attempted to ensure that my own children attended church and catechism classes, but did not feel the necessity nor the commitment to continue on a regular basis. It was more out of an obligation I thought I owed to my children to raise them in a church atmosphere. And yet, I had never really understood it, so I didn't believe I could ever expect them to either.

I recalled that after my divorce from my second husband in 1994, I was so depressed and discouraged, Mom talked me into going to the priest for counseling. No one knew, however, that I was not only struggling with my marriage during this time, but with my failing business and the beginning of serious financial problems, as well. I honestly believed that Father Thomas was going to lay his hands upon the top of my head and immediately relieve me of all my pain and suffering; and that by some miracle God would bless me, and let me win the lottery. Instead Father Thomas asked me if I had been absolved of my sins? Had I asked for forgiveness and served my penance? Did I acknowledge that Jesus was my only Savior and answer to my problems?

What was Father Thomas asking me? I came here to receive his blessing and his help. Didn't he understand I was the victim here? I was the one who had been lied to, stolen from, hurt and humiliated? Didn't anyone understand? I only knew I wanted to "get well" . . . I just didn't know how. I was so confused about who God really was.

Condition . . . of my mind

"Finally, all of you, be like-minded, be sympathetic, love one another, be compassionate and humble. Do not repay evil with evil or insult with insult. On the contrary, repay evil with blessing, because to this you were called so that you may inherit a blessing."

1 Peter 3:8-9

My mind continued to be filled with confusion, fear and uncertainty of the future. I didn't believe that I could possibly ever amount to anything again.

"Hey Friend! Better make sure you don't have any contraband you need to hide," Mattie warned me. "Word is there's a shakedown this morning."

"A shakedown?" I questioned.

"Yea. CO's come through and shake down your bunk and go through your lockbox and all your *sh*. . . Geezz . . . don't you know anything about being locked up, girl?" she asked mockingly.

"No, I really don't" I said under my breath. But I certainly wasn't worried in the least about having anything I shouldn't. It had only been about two weeks since I first arrived at Maryswood, and I still didn't have any money on my books to buy anything; let alone the five dollars needed to purchase a combination safety lock.

I hadn't received any pictures or the prescription contacts I had requested from home. Except for the small paperback Bible I was able to bring inside, I didn't have any books because I had yet to discover that I would have to stand in line for over an hour for the opportunity to go to the library. My only possessions consisted of the initial state-issued clothes, comb, toothbrush, cup, and a few personal items.

After morning inspection, breakfast and cleaning, we were instructed to form a straight line at the side door and proceed to the yard. Nearing the end of October, the wind chill was surprisingly bitter that morning. Attempting to keep my coat zipped up around my neck, hands stuffed into my pockets, and body turned away from the wind as much as possible; I stomped my feet to keep the circulation in my legs going. With nothing other than the heavy coat issued to us, we had nothing else to keep the harsh winter air from whipping through the thin jumpsuits.

Forced to stay in single line formation in the center of the yard, there were no walls to huddle up against to shield the frigid and biting air. Many of the women were expressing very select and descriptive language regarding the weather, for the CO's to hurry up, and that we weren't a herd of cattle out here waiting to go to slaughter!

Finally, after approximately twenty minutes, and wiping my sniffling red nose with the back of my coat sleeve, the whistle blew and we were all marched back inside. The warm air felt so good against my cheeks, and I was reminded of when I had been in grade school and we would be filed back in after a very cold day of recess on the playground.

Scrambling back to my bunk so I could wrap up in my army blanket, I reached the end of my bed . . . and then stood there in total confusion. I looked all around. Was I at the right location? Who moved my lockbox? I was at the correct bed, but my lockbox stood wide open and was filled to the brim with all kinds of lotions, cigarettes, lighters, Little Debbie snacks, razors and numerous other "illegal contraband". I was in an absolute state of panic. Where did all of this come from? Did someone switch boxes on me? I looked around again and grabbed Mattie's arm as she approached our bunk. "Mattie!" I shrieked. "What is all of this? I don't understand!"

"Oooo. Someone got you good girl!" was her only reply.

"What do you mean? This isn't my stuff! I'm not getting into trouble for something someone else did to me!" I insisted.

"Oh, you're going down girl! Someone up in here made sure of that!" she answered. Horrified of what I might be facing, I fell to my knees and started throwing everything out of my box and onto the floor as fast as I could.

"Hey! What do you think you're doing *bi*. . .?! How stupid are you! You want all of us going down for your stupid *sh*..?!" I turned around to see the girl in the bunk immediately to the right standing over top of me. A medium-height, stocky white girl with dirty blond hair, light brown freckles and stern hefty eyebrows, she went by the nickname of "Chopper." The name was very suitable for her as her hair was all chopped off in a "butch" haircut. In addition, she had told me she was serving time for accessory to murder. So naturally I assumed she had probably chopped somebody up.

"But this isn't my stuff! I'm not going to get into trouble for this!" I yelled back at her, not one bit deterred by her loud aggressive approach, and still throwing things on the floor.

"Look here *bi* . . .!" as she grabbed my arm. "Obviously, you don't understand how it works around here. You stupid enough to leave your box unlocked, you deserve to be hit up! Now put everything back in that box! Do it *now*!" she shrieked.

I stood up, turned around to face her, and dropped the few items I had in my hands on the floor; but I didn't pick anything up. Alarmed at my own stubbornness, I firmly stated "You pick it up. I'm done!" I rationalized I was already going to the *hole* for being caught with this unsurmountable amount of contraband, so what did it matter? At least she couldn't beat me up while I was in solitaire.

I hurriedly walked right past Chopper and away from my area while several of the inmates silently stood by looking at me. I didn't want to be in the room when the CO's came to get me, so I proceeded straight to the atrium area and sat in one of the tall wooden chairs lined up against the wall. With arms crossed over my chest and a grim smirk on my face, I just waited.

"Daag girl! Didn't see that coming from *you*!" Red had come to look for me. She had heard of the commotion all the way down at her end of the corridor.

"Yea, well just one more stupid thing I can chalk up to experience," I moan-fully recanted. Realizing everyone had played on my naïve and inexperienced situation, obviously they had all placed their belongings in my unlocked box. More than just being angry, I felt stupid and humiliated for being taken for the fool that I was. My pride was hurt and I felt defeated. Maybe my sister had been right. Maybe I couldn't make it in here.

"Hey, you never really did tell me what you're sitting in here for. I know you said theft, but what 'cha do anyhow?" she persisted. I really didn't want to talk about it to anyone, any more than I had to.

"Embezzlement" I stammered. I could hardly choke out the word. "I stole over $150,000 from a client."

"Whaaaat? You must be sitting pretty! New house, new car, new everything?" Red inquisitively inquired.

"Shoot . . . nothing at all like that. I had my own business for almost four years, but I became so overwhelmed with all the expenses, payroll and taxes. I kept telling myself I was just "borrowing" the money from my client. I kept praying God would let me win the lottery or something so I could pay it all back. Whatever! I'm such an idiot."

Suddenly I realized I had been so angry that the inmates had taken advantage of me. I was furious for believing they would do the right thing and own up to what they had done. I felt betrayed and deceived, bitter and resentful. Now I would have to pay the price for something other people had done to me!

Wow. That revelation hit me right between the eyes. Although I had always felt the guilt and remorse of my crime, I was beginning to wrap my mind around the real truth of what I had done. I had been the victim in many other situations. But not this time. I was the criminal.

. . . but I see another law at work in me, waging war against the law of my mind and making me a prisoner of the law of sin at work within me.

Romans 7:23

We continued to sit there and talk until call was made for lunch. I was confused. Why hadn't they come to get me? "I don't understand Red. Why aren't they looking for me? I'm right here in plain sight."

"I dunno. It is kinda weird," she answered.

We both went back to our bunks to be called in order for the lunch line. Nobody said anything to me as I passed the first several beds to my take my place at my area. Sitting on her bottom bunk, Chopper slightly glanced up at me, and then put her head down and turned away as if to say she actually respected me a little for standing up for myself. Someone had picked up the things I had thrown on the floor, and it appeared as if some of the remaining items in the box might already be gone. I didn't ask anything, and no one offered any indication of what had taken place.

Although I was still very much aware that the CO or sergeant would be coming for me anytime, I proceeded to lunch without any questions or disturbances. I kept peering up from my plate to see if they were searching me out. I could hardly choke down the stale bread lightly spread with peanut butter, and watered-down, lukewarm chicken noodle soup.

Eventually I made my way back to my area, where I discovered literally everything except for pretty much my own personal items had been removed from my lockbox. It was as if nothing had ever happened. I awkwardly climbed up onto my bunk in amazement, and said a silent prayer to God. *"I don't get it God. I don't know what happened, or that it is even over yet, but thank you for your protection of me. I promise I will try not to be so stupid anymore. Please just help me. I have so much to learn."*

I never did hear anything at all about the contraband that had been placed in my box. I reasoned that possibly the CO's knew I was the "new kid" on the block and what had happened. I figured maybe they just brought a trash can and dumped everything into it while we were at lunch. I didn't know or understand any of it, but I knew deep in my heart that God was looking out for me. I couldn't comprehend why, but I was just grateful that He did.

Condition . . . of my heart

"Then you will call on me and come and pray to me, and I will listen to you. You will seek me and find me when you seek me with all your heart. I will be found by you," declares the LORD, *"and will bring you back from your captivity."*

Jeremiah 29:12-14

It was an early Saturday morning. It had been over three weeks now since I had been taken into captivity. "Mail call" the CO shouted from the high platform at the front of the ward. Maybe, just maybe I would receive a letter or something from Don or one of my kids. I knew it would take a while for things to start coming in. But I was so homesick and longed to see or hear something from the outside world. At last . . . "Friend!"

My heart jumped as I scrambled off the bunk and ran up to the platform to retrieve my mail. One single envelope with a return address written in my mother's handwriting. *"Oh, thank you God!"* I just needed to know something, anything at all. I was so lonesome to hear from someone familiar. I quickly opened the envelope that had already been searched by the prison staff before it reached me. There was a note tucked inside from the mailroom that stated $20 had been placed on my books. I was elated. Now I could order some decent shampoo, paper, self-stamped envelopes, pens, Jolly Ranchers. . . and a lock!

The letter from my mother started out tolerable enough, asking how I was, and telling me a few things she and Dad had been doing the past few weeks. However, the very next paragraph began with the shame and guilt they were feeling because of my actions. They couldn't begin to imagine what conceivable thoughts or situations would ever exist that would cause me to do what I had done. She went on to say that she and Dad had always tried to raise me right. Why wouldn't I have just come to them in the very beginning, and possibly they could have helped me? But now I had ruined so many lives. As I continued to read the remainder of the letter, I knew that most of her scolding words were from the pain and stress my parents were trying to deal with right now.

Mom proceeded to tell me that Jen had been staying with them, but they could no longer tolerate her constant crying, staying in her room, not eating anything, and only wanting to see her friends. She continued to explain that Jen was being very disrespectful to them because she had "screamed" at my parents, telling them "You have no idea what I am going through right now!" They told her she had to stay in her room.

My heart was breaking for my daughter. My worst nightmare had come true. I couldn't help her, be there for her, or hold her and tell her everything would be ok. I didn't know how to protect her from everything and everyone. Mom also let me know they were resistant and not pleased in allowing Jennifer to go back home, but Don would just have to deal with her now. They were also very upset with me for not putting my foot down, and insisting she stay with them. Tears rolled down my face. *"Please, just let me be the parent,"* I thought.

She signed the letter *"Love, Mom and Dad"*, but my heart was empty and shattered. I started shaking with the realization that I absolutely had no power, no control, no hope of anything in my life right now. I knew what Jennifer must be going through. What a horrible, horrible feeling to know that everything in your life was at the mercy and discretion of others.

However, knowing deep down that Mom had every reason to be upset; and yet why now, after two long years, had my parents decided to chastise me, when the one thing I needed to hear the most was that as foolish as I had been, that I was still loved and had been forgiven? Why couldn't they be more understanding of Jennifer and what she was going through? I didn't want to hear how they were feeling right now. I couldn't take on everyone's pain all at once. And yet, I knew I had caused this deep anguish.

"Scorn has broken my heart and has left me helpless; I looked for sympathy, but there was none; for comforters, but I found none."

Psalm 69:20

CHAPTER 4

❧ *Conviction* ❧

n: A fixed or firm belief; the state or act of being convicted; the state of being convinced; proven; evidence; an unshakable certainty in something without need of proof or evidence; a final judgment of guilty in a criminal case.

"Because our gospel came to you not simply with words, but also with power, with the Holy Spirit and deep conviction." 1
Thessalonians 1:5

Tuesday was transportation day. Inmates who were being transferred out to either general population within the prison, or possibly to another outside location, would "ride out" to their assigned destination. It was also shower day and library day.

The approximate time to be detained in Admissions was four weeks. It was now drawing close to the time I should be leaving and either escorted to another residence on the grounds, or possibly, hopefully to the Pre-Release Center closer to home. According to some of the women who had previously served time at the Center, I understood I could very possibly qualify to be transported to this medium-security facility. I desperately prayed that I might be eligible to go as I would be so much closer to home and my family; and Don could come to visit me there. "Word" was that although still a state-run prison, the housing and living conditions far surpassed those of the aging and depressed Maryswood facility.

One of the three days a week to take a shower, "Showers in ten minutes! Line up," shouted the CO on duty that morning. Grateful I was closer to the showers than about three-fourths of the dorm, I could be relatively certain there would still be hot water. I hurriedly stripped down, wrapped the large white towel around my body, and poured a small amount of a watered-down shampoo on top of my head. Once we reached the shower area, there would only be three minutes to completely wash and rinse.

As I gradually made my way in line to the showers, I took my place in formation, facing the open stalls. There were approximately twenty stalls, ten on each side of the open tile floor in the shower room. To the ladies already in the showers: "Step out!" A slight pause from the CO on duty, and then "Step in!" to those of us waiting to go in.

Not permitted to have razors to shave, the long dark hair on my legs and armpits were beginning to disgust myself, let alone anyone else. No lotions, make-up, hair-dye, conditioner, or hair spray permitted. No perfume, nail polish, jewelry, hair ties . . . save for the ones the women would make out the elastic they stripped from their socks. Absolutely nothing at all to make you feel that you were any kind of a woman. However, I began to be grateful that I was able to shower at all. I realized my attitude, my outlook, and my demeanor were beginning to change. Thirty days without any amenities, contact, or privileges of any kind, I was very appreciative of what I did receive.

Lined up for the library later that evening, I wanted desperately to read something from the "outside world" to help pass the time. One of the few books I was ever able to check out in Admissions, was a book written by Chuck Coulson regarding the seven months he served in a federal prison for his involvement in the notorious Watergate Scandal of 1972. Once known as former President Nixon's "hatchet man," Colson gained notoriety at the height of the Watergate scandal, and pleaded guilty to obstruction of justice. In 1974, he served time in a federal prison in Alabama as the first member of the Nixon administration to be incarcerated for Watergate-related charges.

I was intrigued by this story as I remembered it very well; occurring several years earlier on June 17th - the very date of my 17th birthday in 1972. Always an enthusiast of true stories of crime, I became more surprised, however, to learn that Colson had become a Christian during the time he was imprisoned. His mid-life conversion to Christianity sparked a radical life change that led to the founding of his non-profit ministry, *Prison Fellowship International*; an international organization that focused on Christian teaching and training to the incarcerated around the world.

Humm . . .I began to surmise, just slightly, maybe there was hope. After all, this guy had been a top government official, a successful businessman in Washington. I could see that even "high-profile" people were very capable of committing "white collar" crimes. I wanted to know more about this man and how he had survived his life after prison.

"For this reason, since the day we heard about you, we have not stopped praying for you. We continually ask God to fill you with the knowledge of his will through all the wisdom and understanding that the Spirit gives."

Colossians 1:9

Few and far between, however, to have the opportunity of obtaining any other books in the library, the paperback Bible I had been able to bring in would soon become the only constant source of any type of reading material available to me. Given to me by my Aunt Bev and Uncle George as a high-school graduation gift, I had never opened the pages, and was completely oblivious of its' content. Difficult to comprehend or acknowledge what possible message of love, forgiveness or promise God could have for me, I persevered to find any kind of hope within its' pages. I didn't know what on earth that could conceivably be; but if there was any, I desperately wanted to find it.

Unaware of the fact that there was an "old" testament and a "new" testament, I couldn't understand why this "Good News" Bible (New Testament only) kept talking about the prophets of years ago. What Prophets? Who were they? And why were Matthew, Mark, Luke and John telling the same story? Regardless, although often difficult to comprehend at times, I did gather enough understanding from the actual words spoken from Jesus that He truly did love me. I learned that His love was so great He paid the ultimate price for me… a sinner, a criminal. He didn't do anything to deserve what I had chosen to do, and yet He suffered indescribable and inhumane cruelty of beatings, torture and eventual death on a cross, so that I may have a new life.

"Jesus straightened up and asked her, "Woman, where are they? Has no one condemned you?" "No sir, not one," she said. "Then neither do I condemn you," Jesus declared. "Go now and leave your life of sin."

John 8:10-11

Stop the Insanity

From the moment I walked through the heavy metal doors of the prison, I didn't feel that I "belonged" there. I felt that I was so much better than "they" (inmates) were. No question I still did what was asked of me, but I resented being treated like a "common criminal." Couldn't anyone see that I had made a horrible mistake, but I was not a "bad" person? My thoughts were not filled with "evil" thoughts, and I had never set out to purposely destroy anyone.

Overwhelmed with the huge financial responsibility of running my own business, I had somehow convinced myself that I was just "borrowing" the money. Never in my wildest dreams did I ever think to myself that I was actually stealing anything. My plan had always been to "pay back every dime ."

Soon after the realization that I was deeply in debt in both my personal and professional life, I continued to assure myself that I would be able to "fix" everything. I would just work harder . . . more hours, more jobs. I would obtain more clients, hire more people, market my company, and acquire more accounts. If I could just borrow enough money to keep the doors open and the rent paid, I would not be a failure. I would rise above everyone's pre-conceived notion that my personal life of yet another divorce, bankruptcy, and loss of all I had, would prove to be mistaken at best. With three of my four children still living at home during the initial years, counting on me to be their provider, caregiver, and protector of the world; how could I possibly accept anything other than I would somehow take care of them?

But as much as I had wanted to live in denial, change the course of destiny, and reject anything that would ultimately lead to my total downfall, I would eventually have to bring myself to face the hard truth. I was a lying, irrational and crooked convict indeed. I had embezzled literally thousands of dollars over a period of eighteen months from my largest client. It was too inconceivable that I could possibly even reason this in my mind. Why didn't I just stop the insanity? Was there something about me that I just couldn't face the inevitable?

"For by the grace given me I say to every one of you: Do not think of yourself more highly than you ought, but rather think of yourself with sober judgment, in accordance with the faith God has distributed to each of you."

Romans 12:3

Eventually I had to face reality and come to terms with everything. I could not even begin to imagine how I could possibly pay everyone back anymore. Upon opening my own business several years prior, I had taken out bank loans, personal loans, and cashed in my share of the retirement fund from my first marriage. I had purchased office furniture and equipment on credit with major office supply companies, and charged many supplies and services to credit cards. I was overwhelmed with payroll, taxes, insurance and benefits for my employees; as well as the upkeep and maintenance of office equipment and computers. During the initial years of this start-up company, I had approached my "then" in-laws and borrowed $10,000 to begin this venture I once believed would be a huge success. By this time, however, my now (second) ex-husband was taking me to court to sue me for the money that was owed to his parents. The phone was ringing daily from the landlord, debt collectors, business owners, and vendors requiring down payments for upcoming events.

The guilt and stress of trying to stay ahead of all of the endless bills, year-end audits, monthly financial reports and bank statements finally broke me. I began to withdraw from reality and everyone around me. I would mask the façade and go to work every day; only to come home, draw the curtains, and turn all the lights out. I would curl up in the farthest corner of the couch, cover up in the safety and comfort of a blanket, and turn on the television to a movie or program; desperately seeking to escape the outside world and what was before me. I quit going to Jen's games, or any public events I could possibly avoid. I dreaded going to the grocery store, bank or gas station. I tried to avoid looking at anyone at all. I was certain they could see the guilt, the sin, and the shame all over my face. Other than the darkness of my own home, I would only go to the bars late at night with Don, hoping to drink away my fears and agony.

The Plan

By the end of the summer and now September of 1997, I knew the end was near. I had completely drained every dime out of my client's account. There was no turning back time for me. Once again, in my attempt to "control" everything, I devised a "plan of action." I had lied to, stolen from, and made empty promises to my victim, my children, and so many others for the last time. I couldn't do and be all the things I had wanted to be for everyone. I had failed at my position of trust and leadership of my own company. I had deceived a very important client, literally stealing thousands of dollars I knew deep down that I could never repay. At long last, I surmised the only answer to make things right again was to end my life forever.

I had made the decision several months prior to purchase a life insurance policy of $250,000 for myself. I now trusted I could pull this off to make it appear to be an accident so the coverage would be paid. Just enough to pay off my victim, my debts, and leave some money for my children; I felt more than ever that I owed this to all of them. It was the only answer. I also reasoned that my children would not be strong enough to face the ugly truth of what their mother had done. I believed they would hate me forever. At least if I was gone, maybe they could still find it in their hearts to love me.

I had written my final letters to my parents and my three oldest children, explaining everything in detail. I begged them to please forgive me, and to understand why I had to do this. I pleaded with them that they would not share my plan, knowing the insurance company would not cover death by suicide. I just couldn't face the brutal truth of what I had done, nor face the people I had betrayed and hurt to such a great extent; much less accept the facts regarding all legal matters, trials, prison and publicity of my crime.

Although I knew Jen would be devastated and heartbroken, as well as to be forced to leave her home, school and friends; I would be sure enough money was left behind to ensure she had all the *things* she needed. I also knew that although her father had never really been around from the time she had been a baby, I also knew that he loved her, and would make certain she would be well taken care of. Certainly, leaving money to take care of everything was the absolute answer to every situation now. Maybe somehow, someday everyone would forgive me.

I also left explicit, detailed instructions to ensure the large debt owed to my client would be compensated in full, funeral expenses paid, and the remaining funds to be distributed to my four children. I was convinced, and surprisingly very much at peace regarding my decision to end my life that day. I wasn't afraid anymore. I knew everything would be okay now. After all, I was back in control again.

The Voice

"Go home to your family and tell them how much the Lord has done for you, and how He has had mercy on you."

Mark 5:19

Traveling eastbound on I-370 toward Zionville, at a speed of approximately 85-90 miles per hour, I had planned the exact time and place of where I would deliberately crash my white 1991 Ford Aerostar mini-van. Definitely not wanting to hurt anyone else however, my plan was to make it appear that I had "fallen asleep" at the wheel. I continued to drive, and remained steadfast until there was no other traffic on the road. As I traveled further down the six-lane highway, I suddenly realized there were thick concrete 4-5 foot "walls" that periodically divided the interstate down the center. This was perfect. I would steer into the huge barriers and be killed instantly. There would not be a chance that I could travel onto the other side of the highway into on-coming traffic.

The only vehicle still remaining on the road however, was a large semi-truck. I couldn't seem to navigate away from it. So eventually I accelerated and was so close to the truck, the front of my vehicle was positioned almost directly underneath the tail end of the huge red and silver sixteen-wheeler. Astonished at the peace and tranquility I was feeling, as well as the calmness of the anticipation of what was about to happen; I closed my eyes, laid my head against the steering wheel, and pressed on the pedal with great force.

Instantly what sounded like a loud booming voice declared, *"What do you think you are doing?"* Startled, I opened my eyes in utter amazement, sensing there must be someone in the car with me.

"What!? Who's there? Who is that?" I looked about in total disbelief. At that same instant I realized the trailer-truck had traveled almost half-a-mile down the highway and was about to crest the top of a large hill. How could this be? Had I been dreaming? Had I truly fallen asleep for an instant? I *know* that truck was just inches in front of me a few seconds ago!

Again, in a softer, yet firm voice, *"What do you think you are doing?"* I realized now the voice was not an audible voice, but one that I heard in my mind. In complete astonishment, I concluded now it could only be God Himself.

Certain that I must be hallucinating, I answered *"But, God, we talked about this. We planned this all out."*

The voice in my head continued, *"No, you planned all of this. This was YOUR decision."* I knew it was true. I was only trying to convince myself that this was the only and right thing I could do - for everyone involved.

God's voice persisted *"What are you doing to your children? They have already lost one parent. And what are you doing to your parents? They have already lost a daughter. This will destroy your mother."*

I knew my mother had suffered immeasurable loss when one of my younger sisters, Beffie, had taken her own life at the age of 27. It had been ten years now since our mother had become severely distraught, and prescribed medication for severe depression. I knew that for her to endure yet another daughter committing suicide would be excruciatingly painful for her.

I now understood that God was speaking to me through my conscious mind, but His words were still very bold and real to me. *"But what do you want me to do, God? How can I fix this?"*

In a very quiet but convincing voice now; *"You are to turn around and go home. You need to tell your family everything and turn yourself in. You need to take responsibility for what you have done."*

Answering quietly, *"I know it's the right thing to do, but I am so scared, God. Please, please don't make me do this. I'm so afraid."*

Very softly and lovingly, just as a Father's voice should be, *"I know you are."* He further explained, *"I promise you I will be with you every step of the way. Do not be afraid. I will protect you."* At that instant I knew that somehow, I was going to get through this. The peace …the very *real* and true peace that came over me, was indescribable. I felt a love I had never experienced before. I *KNEW* that God had spoken to me. I was humbled and meek at His presence. He had made Himself known to me.

I had become extremely depressed, withdrawn, and had reached the end all of my life. I was suicidal, truly believing death was my only escape, when God literally spoke, and breathed life back into my heart and soul.

"And I will give them a heart to know me, that I am the Lord; and they shall be my people, and I will be their God; for they shall return unto me with their whole heart."

Jeremiah 24:7

The Horrible Truth

That very afternoon I called Don and asked him to please leave work and come to the house. I had something terribly important I needed to tell him. A tall slender man with thick stylish, although completely silver hair; Don was a handsome and virile man. His confident swagger and demeanor were especially attractive to me. I always told him he reminded me of

Clint Eastwood, or the late actor, James Dean; most especially when he would work or talk with a cigarette dangling from the side of his mouth, his eyebrows drawn together in a serious concentration of what he was doing, or about to say.

When he arrived at the house, he stood just inside the door. "What's wrong? You're scaring me" Don's shaky voice questioned.

In a similar trembling voice, I quietly offered, "I won't blame you if you leave me and never want to see me again. I'm so ashamed."

A moment of silence, and then he asked "Please tell me what you're talking about. What happened?" I could see the fear in his eyes and the sweat on his forehead from the dread of the unknown.

"I'm so sorry Don. I love you, but I have to take care of some things that I have gotten myself into. I don't even know where to begin. All I know is I can't go on like this anymore."

I found myself spilling out the whole story; the whole horrible, shocking truth. When I was done, I could only imagine what his reaction might be. "I knew there's been something wrong with you for a while now. I couldn't figure out what it was, but you've been so different," Don calmly stated as he stood up and began pacing nervously back and forth across the living room. He pulled out a cigarette and lit it up. "Do your parents or kids know? Does anyone know?" his voice quivering as he wiped the sweat from his brow.

"No. I couldn't tell anyone something as terrible as this. Only that Tina has been asking me some accounting questions at the office. I know she has suspected something is wrong for a while now. I just keep telling her I'll take care of it. I don't know how much she might really know."

I explained that vendors had been calling, asking for their money, and I had wondered if they had contacted the president of the Association we were contracted with. "I really don't know who knows what, if anything at all. I just know I have to bring an end to it. I know I will go to jail. I know I have to turn myself in."

Taking a deep breath, Don quietly asked "Why don't we go talk to your parent's first so we can at least let them know what is going to happen? Let's see if they can help in any way at all. You need to get an attorney first before you do anything." Astonished, I realized that Don really did love me. He had already been helping me with bills and rent money. I had truly expected him to be angry and walk out of my life forever. It would have killed me, but I wouldn't have blamed him at all.

I let Jennifer know we were going to Grandma and Grandpa's, and would be home later. "Are you okay, Mom? Is everything ok?" I knew my depressive mood, swollen eyes and tear-stained face was very obvious to her.

"I'm fine, honey. Everything will be okay, I promise. Make sure you do your homework and I'll call you pretty soon." As I walked out the door, I wondered if I was trying to convince her, or myself. *"Oh God, what will happen to her if I am arrested tomorrow?"* I was sick to my stomach with the thought of it.

Breaking the news to my parents was devastating. My Mom sobbed, and just kept saying "No, no. This can't be happening. Where have we gone so wrong?" My heart was heavy with shame and disgrace as I watched her small body shaking with disbelief. I knew I was breaking her heart all over again. How much more was she expected to take? After the loss of my sister Beffie, as well as so many other horrific situations within our family, my mother appeared damaged and defeated. I couldn't bear that I was placing yet another life-shattering episode in her life.

In a calm, yet logical tone "Have you contacted your client to let them know?" my father asked.

Sitting at the kitchen table with my head in my hands, I shook my head and quietly answered "No."

"Well, I think you better do that just as soon as possible. You need to take care of as much as you can before tomorrow." As much as I resented so many things about my father's demeanor, he could also be realistic, and believed in tackling everything head on.

Very hesitantly, I dialed the number to the treasurer of the association. It was almost 10:00pm. It would be 9:00pm in Wisconsin where Bob lived. Bob was well into his seventies, maybe even eighties. A small frail man, he was the kindest, wisest and most loving man I knew. He had traveled almost eight hours from out-of-state every month for two years to go over all the bills, invoices and bank statements, as well as to sign checks for payments. In addition, he always left a few "emergency" blank, signed checks in case there was an immediate need to pay a bill when he wasn't there. He trusted me completely.

"Hello," a quavering voice answered the phone.

Very quietly I began, "Hi, Bob. This is Nanette. I am really sorry to call you so late, but I need to tell you something."

"I'm sorry. What?" he quietly asked. I repeated myself a little louder. A long silence and then "Are you okay?" he asked me.

With a trembling voice I responded "No . . . I don't even know how to tell you this." I couldn't go on with the conversation. I started to break down crying.

"Nan . . . what is wrong? Please tell me."

"I'm so sorry Bob. I can't even tell you." Again, another long silence as I trembled and cried.

And then very sympathetically, Bob asked "How much?"

Startled, I asked "What?"

Bob continued "How much?" Somehow, he knew.

"A lot. It's a lot." I was mortified.

After a brief silence, "Oh, honey. I just put over fifty thousand dollars into my projects (low-income housing), or I would have given it to you."

"*What?*" I thought to myself. "*Did he NOT just hear what I said to him?*"

"I don't understand. I stole a lot of money Bob. I am so sorry."

I was in total shock, and yet I now understood when God said He would stay with me every step of the way. He helped me get through telling my boyfriend, my parents and now the treasurer - of whom I had just admitted I had forged his signature on some of the checks; and now placed him in the midst of a dreadful and disgraceful investigation.

"Have you called Ron yet?" he asked. Ron was the President of the Association.

"No, I am going to call him in the morning. Then I will turn myself in. I'm sorry. I'm so sorry, Bob. I know you hate me."

Very calmly Bob continued "Listen to me. I don't hate you. You talk to Ron first, and then call me after you talk to him. Try to get some rest."

"Ok, I will. Bob, I'm sorry. I'm so ashamed."

He said "Get some rest" before he hung up the phone. I realized this was the worst thing I ever had to do that I could recall, and yet I was somewhat relieved it was finally over.

Gentle Spirit

I couldn't sleep all night knowing what I would have to face the next day. I said goodbye to Jennifer in the morning, not knowing if I would see her that evening. I went into the office extra early to get things in order. As they arrived one by one, I called my staff of five into the conference room for a meeting. Not able to look anyone in the eye, I stammered out that we were closed effective immediately, and there was no money available to disburse payroll or insurance benefits. Everyone was understandably distraught and infuriated with me. After many questions, apologies and the suggestion they should go immediately to the unemployment office, the staff left in total distress and disbelief.

The first of much turmoil and heartache to come within the next several weeks, I then placed an urgent call to the president of the association. Ron immediately made the 30-minute drive to the office. When he arrived, he stood inside the door and asked "What's going on Nanette?" I sat at the receptionist desk at the front door with head held in my hands, shook my head back and forth, and couldn't even answer him. "Had better days?" he offered to ease the tension. Taking off his coat, he set his briefcase down and calmly took a seat in the chair in front of the desk.

I took a deep breath and, once again, found myself spilling out the whole horrific story; while offering total cooperation and remorse for my actions. Ron explained that he had been receiving phone calls from vendors and members of the association stating that I had not been taking their calls; and there appeared to be several unpaid bills. After continued discussion, Ron finally announced he was leaving now. Perplexed, I asked if he wasn't going to call the police and have me arrested. "Do you want me to have you arrested?" he asked.

"No" as I shook my head and questioned his intentions.

"Well, you stated you would be cooperative, and as long as you're willing to work with us, I see no reason to call the police. I will have to contact the board members, as well as an attorney. Just stay in touch, and we will see what the next steps will be." With that, Ron stepped forward and slightly hugged me. He said "Look, you're going to get through this. Everything is going to be ok."

Once again, there was that forgiveness, that gentle spirit, that unconditional, non-judgmental mindset that I couldn't comprehend. Did he not just understand everything I had told him? And he was just leaving me here? Who does that? Then I knew. God does that. He had promised to be with me through every step of the way. I then understood that these men knew and recognized the trust and love of a God far more than I ever thought possible.

I locked the doors of the office and went home. I couldn't bear any phone calls that day. I knew I had to go back over the next several days and clean everything out; but I needed time to recollect my thoughts. Eventually the landlord, vendors, office equipment companies, and others I owed money to, came to look for me. Shortly thereafter, I was contacted by a detective at the police department to come to the station and answer some questions.

Prayers on my Pillow

"Count!" the night shift CO announced. It was ten o'clock. I was grateful for the opportunity to be required to be on our bunks and be quiet. The women had been especially loud and filled with relentless, obnoxious energy that evening. I thought to myself, *"Is there not even one person in this place that can speak an entire sentence without using every curse word imaginable?"* Finally, able to have some rest after count, I rolled up my usual "pillow" of my winter coat, and lay down to read my paperback Bible until the lights went out at eleven o'clock.

Night after night, I would wrestle with the depression, anxiety and fear of each day, and seek to realize some form of relief from reading the stories about Jesus. Over time, I would come to begin to understand more and more the accounts written by the disciples, and eventually the written words of promise, truth, and subsequent peace that would provide some form of comfort to me. As time went on, I would come to anxiously await for each night to begin so I could crawl into my "safe" place and be with God. Ultimately each night, I would finally fall asleep, faithfully awaiting the next morning so I could mark another day served, off of my tiny laminated calendar.

"I anticipated the dawning of the morning, and cried: I hoped in thy words. Mine eyes anticipated the night-watches, that I might meditate on thy word."

Psalm 119:147-148

Alone and isolated from the outside world, I knew that God hadn't sent me to prison. That was of my own poor choosing. But I did know that He had a purpose for *allowing* me to be convicted for my crime. For only here, in this secluded atmosphere, did He have my one-hundred percent attention. For only here would I truly turn to Him for true conviction of my heart and soul.

Chapter 5

❧ *Determination* ❧

n: Firmness of purpose; resolve; a fixed intention or resolution; the ascertaining or fixing of the quantity, quality, position, or character of something; the act of making or arriving at a decision; the settling of a question or case by an authoritative decision or pronouncement, especially by a judicial body; the decision or pronouncement made.

"All this I tested by wisdom and I said, "I am determined to be wise — but this was beyond me."

Ecclesiastes 7:23

When I returned home from work that cool fall afternoon of 1997, there was a message to contact Detective Biggs to come in for questioning. My heart skipped a beat and that sick feeling in the pit of my stomach returned. My hand trembling, I dialed the phone number. When the detective answered the phone and requested that I come in that very evening, I asked if I would be taken into custody at that time. My voice shaking in fear and anticipation, I wanted to know if I would need to make arrangements for Jennifer if I would not be coming home that night. "You have not been formally charged with anything at this time, and I understand you stated that you are willing to cooperate. Is that still the case Ms. Friend?"

"Yes sir. I'm not denying anything, and I will fully cooperate. I just want to take care of my daughter" I blurted out.

"I understand. Come on in and we will discuss it. If you are willing to cooperate and agree to let us know where you are, we will see how things go," he answered.

As I walked into his small dark office, with two brown hard-plastic molded chairs positioned in front of his desk, I immediately noticed a large wooden cross attached to the wall immediately behind his seat. I instantly felt a sense of relief. Detective Biggs walked around the desk to greet me and held out his hand to shake mine with a firm, but gentle grip. "Hello Ms. Friend. Thank you for coming in. We'll try not to take up too much of your time." Again, I felt a little better thinking I must be going home if I could trust his statement.

The detective was a medium height, slender black man. His appearance was professional and handsome, with a well-groomed dark black beard and mustache. Dressed in a white button-down collar shirt, navy blue tie and dark suit pants; his demeanor was gentle, but confident. He made me feel at ease, and that I could trust his word. After several hours of questioning, handwriting analysis, and promises made to report any changes of address, phone number, or work hours; I was told my case would now be taken to the grand jury for possible indictment. I would then receive a letter regarding formal charges if recommended by the grand jury, and that I would be required to attend an arraignment hearing. I further understood I would have to face my charges, and plead on my own behalf of guilty or not. "Do you have an attorney, Ms. Friend?"

"No sir" I answered.

"Well you are entitled to an attorney, and the court will appoint one for you if you cannot afford one. We'll be in touch. You have a nice evening and we're going to get through this together, okay?'

"Yes sir. Thank you." I stammered out.

Once again, I was in total disbelief that yet another person was so nice, so compassionate, and was not placing hand-cuffs on me. Is this how it is, God? Are there actually kind and forgiving people in the world? I certainly did not understand it at all, but I was incredibly thankful I could go home. I cried as I drove home that cold and rainy night. I wasn't sure if it was due to the relief I felt to finally go home, or of what I knew I still had to face. I decided it was likely a little of both.

A few weeks later, I had been able to leave the arraignment hearing on my own recognizance, and complete paperwork to request a court-appointed attorney. When it became public knowledge and printed in the local newspaper regarding my third-degree felony charges of aggravated theft (non-violent, but an extensive amount of money over an extended period of time) and forgery; I immediately lost my job as a customer service representative at a local company I had been working for through a temporary agency. However, I was soon able to secure a good job in another city about forty-five minutes away. I hated the long drive, working in sales, and the constant fear of the company finding out about my crime; but I felt fortunate, and a lot more comfortable working in a place where no one knew me.

Angel on the Wall

It had been just over two years since the whole process of the entire investigation and legal proceedings had begun. Now the fall of 1999, at long last the day of the final hearing and sentencing had been set. I was to report to the courthouse at 8:30am on Thursday morning. I spoke with my attorney the previous Tuesday afternoon. "Are you sure I will be coming home after court and not have to serve any time?" I asked

Katherine, my court-appointed attorney. "Because if that's not the case, then I need to let my workplace know, and get all of my belongings tomorrow."

"No, no you will be back at work that very afternoon. It has been decided and agreed upon between the victim, the prosecutors, your parole officer and myself. Official recommendation has already been made to the judge, and the judge most always goes with what is recommended. Don't worry about anything at all. You will only have to serve five years of probation, and make restitution to the victim. It is what they have requested."

I had been completely astonished when I first learned that the Association I had stolen the money from had held a special meeting and requested the courts that I not serve any prison time; only that I should obtain a job and make restitution payments to them. I thought back to my attempt to end my life in the van that dreadful day when God first made himself known to me. He promised He would stand beside me and get me through this every step of the way. Was it possible that all of these people collectively had their heart softened by this almighty God? It didn't make one bit of sense to me at all. Why had they not just had me arrested and thrown away the key? Maybe I could somehow live with myself if they just hated me and were unforgiving. Still, I had my doubts and kept waiting for the shoe to drop.

I drove myself to the courthouse that October Thursday morning. I didn't want, or feel the need to have anyone come with me. I knew I would be leaving right after the hearing. Directed to take my place at the table in the courtroom, I couldn't help but stare up at the larger-than-life, hand-painted beautiful Angel brushed directly on the wall over the Judge's bench. I was so nervous I was shaking; however, the sight of the angelic creation gave me some form of comfort. Once again, that symbolic presence to let me know that God was with me every step of the way, just as He had promised. Waiting for the judge to enter the courtroom, and as Katherine explained last minute details of what to expect; I found myself looking up at the Angel and asking God for His divine intervention.

Because I had been assured all along that I would never serve any prison time, I never told Jennifer or anyone other than my parents, Don and my three oldest children about what had happened. I never made any arrangements, signed over temporary custody or power-of-attorney papers, or made any plans at all for my daughter. I wasn't prepared in any way. I softly whispered to myself *"God, if I have to go to prison, can I please be able to go home and tell my family and Jennifer before I leave? I need to have some time to get everything ready."* Then I found myself surprised for even having those thoughts, when I had been adamantly reassured, and confident I would be going home after court. I would later understand that God had been preparing me for what was to come.

"All rise." The bailiff announced the entrance of the judge into the courtroom. After all charges, details of the crime, specific stipulations and final recommendations of the case were read and discussed, the judge asked if I had anything to say to the court. All of a sudden, I was remarkably nervous and tense. My throat was as dry as sand, and I became extremely choked up and couldn't utter a word. It was like someone was squeezing the air out of me and I couldn't breathe. I could barely get out a horrible attempt to say "I'm sorry. I'm so sorry."

The bailiff announced again to please rise for the sentencing. The presiding Judge waited a moment more, and then stated "While I realize you are sorry and that all recommendations have indicated you should be able to serve your time strictly on probation, I feel that I would not be a very good judge and be extremely remorse if I did not find you guilty of aggravated theft and forgery. I therefore decree that you shall serve a one-year mandatory prison sentence at the Women's State Correctional Institute at Maryswood."

There it was. The shoe had fallen . . . hard. I knew it was too good to be true. I didn't know what to say or do. I couldn't even move. I must have misunderstood what the judge had said. My attorney and probation officer, Lisa, both looked at me in bewilderment. Katherine shook her head and whispered we would appeal it immediately. But then, curiously, the judge called the prosecutor and Katherine to his bench. I couldn't hear or understand what they were whispering. I was still in shock, and that moment was all a blur to me. I felt like all the blood had drained out of my body and that none of this could be real. I watched as the bailiff walked to the side of the room and faced me with handcuffs in his hands. I thought I was going to pass out. I prayed desperately that the judge had decided to table his decision, and shelve my sentence in the event I should violate my probation in any way during the five-year period. Eventually the attorneys returned to their seats, and Katherine softly placed her hand on top of mine.

Judge Markowitz repeated himself, "Ms. Friend. I have made the final decision that you will serve a one-year mandatory sentence at the Women's State Petitionary at Maryswood. It is my belief that you will never be able to make full restitution to your victim, and therefore you must serve time to make some form of payment for your crime to your victim and society." He paused again and then continued, "However, I will grant you permission to go home to your family to explain to them what will take place, as well as to provide you with the time to make any necessary arrangements you may need to make. You are to report to the County Correction Center at 9:00am Monday morning to begin your sentence at that time. Do you have any questions?"

"No sir. Thank you," my meek voice quivering.

Katherine and Lisa quickly escorted me out of the courtroom and into the lobby area. They directed me to sit on the bench until they returned. I sat out there all by myself in total disbelief of what had just happened. My legs were shaking and I kept wrenching my hands together so tightly. I had to keep telling myself to just breathe. But then I remembered my prayer about going home to tell my family. I couldn't comprehend all of this, but I was profoundly aware that God had heard my prayer. Then at that moment, a compelling sense of peace came over me that I could not understand or explain; but I sorely felt that everything was somehow going to be okay.

Katherine and Lisa came back through the large stained-glass doors of the courtroom. "Okay, we have asked for an emergency hearing with the judge at 8:00am on Monday morning. We explained to him that the only reason you pled guilty to the charges was because we told you to do so, not because you wanted to. We have explained that we will ask for a trial hearing." I just sat there and looked at them. "Are you okay? You look like you have seen a ghost," Katherine asked me.

Very softly, I answered her. "No. No, I don't want to go to trial. This has already taken over two years of my life waiting, wondering and worrying. I did it and I'm not going to say I didn't. I just want to do what is right and get on with my life. A trial could take another two to three years, and I can't go through this anymore. I'm not changing it."

Both my attorney and probation office looked at each other and then sat next to me on the bench, one on either side. Katherine said, "Well, we've already asked for the time. So, why don't you take the next few days and think about it. If that's still what you want, then that's what we'll do. Meanwhile, spend some time with your family." Then as an afterthought, she added "Which by the way, do you understand what just happened in there?"

I looked at her with a puzzled look on my face. "Yes. I was sentenced to one year at Maryswood."

"No. I mean, do you understand that when someone is sentenced to go to prison, you are cuffed and taken away immediately. *No one* ever gets to go home and spend time with their family and get things ready before they leave. Never in the twelve years that this judge has served, have I ever seen anyone get to go home. I can't believe that!"

Lisa shook her head in agreement and said "No, that *never* happens!" It was confirmed. God had heard my prayer. And somehow, I was okay with it now. As I took a deep breath, I finally felt some form of relief that I could see an end in sight. I knew it was very strange, but I now understood it was all the waiting that had been slowly wearing me down. But now there was an answer – one way or the other, but an answer none-the-less. I now knew that I was more determined than ever to get through this, and get on with my life.

'This is what the Lord, the God of your father David, says: 'I have heard your prayer and seen your tears; I will heal you.'
2 Kings 20:5

Emotional Faces

"Friend! Front and center!" Called to the CO's desk, I was instructed to report immediately to the prison psychologist. I was feeling especially pleased because I knew the psychologist was one of the exiting appointments. It was my fourth week in "Admissions," and I was hopeful this interview would help determine the possibility of being transported out to the Pre-Release Center.

Arriving at her office at the front of the building, I was well aware this scheduled time was a matter of determining what was going on in my criminal mind, and to what extent I was going to own up to it. Actually, I was somewhat relieved to have the opportunity to finally speak with someone about everything. Possibly *she* could help me understand my irrational and unethical behavior these past few years. Over the previous three years, my life had grown to a state of becoming extremely out of control. I am not sure I could possibly explain my exact state of mind to her. I didn't even know who that person was anymore. Somehow, I had lost all sense of "normal" perception.

On the wall of the doctor's office was a large poster with several different "emotional" faces on it. Under each face was a word describing each expression. The psychologist asked me to review the poster and pick out the "face" that would best describe my feelings at that moment.

I reviewed each one carefully, contemplating several of the choices. By process of elimination, I certainly didn't feel "happy," "confident," or "hopeful." Possibly I felt "overwhelmed", "embarrassed" or even "anxious." I *knew* I felt "guilty", "ashamed" and "frightened". I considered how my life was about to drastically and forever change. Thinking back . . . mentally, financially, and spiritually broken, I had somehow convinced myself that my pathetic and destructive lifestyle was not hurting anyone else but myself.

Eventually, the most prominent face that caught my attention was "determined". I thought of the young girl doing push-ups in boot camp the first week I arrived at the prison. I knew it took a lot of determination and purpose for her to continue on with the program, despite how difficult and grueling it was. When I announced my decision, the psychologist asked why I had chosen that particular feeling. I explained I didn't understand why I had made so many poor and senseless choices in my life, but I was determined to find out. I was intent to change the things in my life that had eventually destroyed me and my family.

"Have you accepted responsibility for the crime you have committed?" *Humm. . .* there was that question again. I thought back to my conversation with Father Thomas. Had *I* accepted responsibility for what *I* had done? I mean, I guess I had. I had admitted to my crime. And yet I realized right then I really hadn't... *I couldn't.* That would mean admitting and accepting everything I had ever done was my fault.

I wanted to console myself somewhat by justifying what I had done was because of the pain and harm others had caused me throughout my life. Didn't she understand that if my father, ex-relationships, and other men in my life had not abused, beaten, cheated on, or in other ways mistreated me, I would have never been forced to do the things I did? This wasn't fair. Why should I have to pay for the sins of others? I wanted to believe that if all the awful and terrible things in my life had not happened to me, I would have never reached this state of total chaos and instability. After all, certainly I was the victim. Had I built this wall of protection around me that made me think I could keep all of the lies, pain, and things I couldn't control out of my life?

The psychologist went on to tell me that I was suffering from an addiction. She continued to explain that addiction was not always a habit or compulsion. Often when we feel threatened, lose control, or are no longer able to cope with a situation; we find dependence, or a "need" that we can fulfill and be in control of. I was clearly confused by this time. I understood I had not been rational in my thinking what-so-ever. But this was not a way of life for me. I had hoped she could explain to me what it was within me that had somehow precluded me from believing, accepting, or admitting that what I had been doing or thinking during this time was so terribly wrong.

She continued on with several different case scenarios which seemed to make some sense to me. Regardless, I had chosen "determined," so I told myself I had to accept what she was telling me. I did realize, however, more than anything, I had to make some drastic changes in my way of thinking. I desperately needed a "higher" power to guide me. . . I needed Jesus. I just didn't know it yet.

November 14th

It was my oldest daughter, Jodi's 23rd birthday. Jodi had been especially heartbroken when I left. She had cried uncontrollably when I said my good-byes to everyone. Her husband tried to console her, but she was shaking so bad. My heart ached for her as well. She had been working for me at the office prior to my downfall, and I had to let her go just like everyone else. I had failed her miserably.

I had finally started to receive letters from my kids. Everyone seemed to be doing as well as could be expected. They were each telling me what was going on with their work and their kids. Jen had moved back home with Don, and assured me they were making it work. I longed to hear their voices. I was so homesick.

I had written that we were not permitted to make phone calls to home until we had been there for 30 days, but that was now only five days away and I found someone who was willing to let me use her ten-minute "phone time." I asked everyone if they could all be at Jodi's house the night of her birthday, and I would call there at 7:00pm.

The night finally came and I had knots in my stomach waiting for the appointed time I could use the phone. I was also extremely nervous that someone would "rat" me out for using the phone *illegally*. Finally, it was 7:00 o'clock. I jumped up off the chair I had been waiting in and took my turn to dial the number. I could hear the *ringing* on the other end, and anxiously awaited for someone to answer.

"Hello?" It was Jodi. I immediately started to cry.

"Happy birthday honey. I'm so sorry to have to miss your birthday, but I love and miss you so much." I continued to sob at the sound of her voice.

"Are you ok Mom?"

"Yes, I'm good. Really, I am. I'm ok. How are the boys?" I inquired.

"They're good. Jacob doesn't understand why he can't see Grandma right now. We told him you were at work." Once again, I couldn't even begin to imagine how everyone was coping about what to say to others regarding where I was. I felt horrible.

"Is Jill, or Jennifer, or Jamie there? I only have ten minutes. I love you and happy birthday."

"Yes, Jill's right here. I'll let you talk to her next. I love you Mom" as I could hear her continue to cry. I was overwhelmed with emotion as I continued to talk to everyone for a few minutes. I spoke with Don and cried even more. As my time was coming to an end, I became so chocked up I could hardly speak.

"I'm still in Admissions and don't know where I will go from here. I can only let you know once I find out. The phone's going to shut me off in a minute. I'm sorry. I'm really sorry. I love you." I hung up and went to my bunk and sobbed. My heart was breaking. Red came down and tried to console me. "I need to get out of here. I miss my family so much."

"I know you do. But you're going to get through this" Red whispered.

CHAPTER 6

❧ *Realization* ❧

n: The act of realizing or the condition of being realized; to conceive vividly as real; to be fully aware of; to bring into concrete existence; to accomplish, gain or effort.

"Be sober, be vigilant; because your adversary the devil walks about like a roaring lion, seeking whom he may devour. Resist him, steadfast in the faith, knowing that the same sufferings are experienced by your brotherhood in the world."

1 Peter 5:8-9 NKJV

It was Tuesday once again, and now just over 30 days since I first heard the loud clicking noise of steel locks denying me access to the outside world. I had anticipated my name would be called that morning and had gathered my things in preparation of the move. After breakfast and mail call, I anxiously awaited as they announced the list of those women leaving that particular morning. However, I was sorely disappointed when my name was not among those called to *pack it up* for transportation. I would have to stay in Admissions at least another week. As an overabundance of pregnant women transported in every week, it soon became clear these were always the first to be transferred out.

Pamela, the quiet young black girl in the lower bunk immediately to my left, had been approved and assigned to the boot camp. I wished her luck and told her she could do this!

I would be watching for her out on the lawn. Deep inside, my heart ached to be able to walk out the doors with her.

Peaches 'n Cream

The new inmates brought in that day were sitting out in the atrium area on the metal folding chairs. Almost immediately the whispers of gossip among the women were making the rounds regarding the newbies that week. One woman of rather troubling nature seemed to be of particular interest to everyone. "Did you see her? She's back!"

"Ooohh . . . *hell no*! I hope she don't even get close to me!" another echoed.

Obviously, someone of concern, I soon overheard this woman's name to be "Peaches", and that she had returned after having just left Maryswood approximately six months prior. I quietly wondered if *Peaches* was her legal birth name, or just a nickname she went by. I was not "prison smart" enough yet to realize that several of the inmates went by nicknames. Regardless, I didn't particularly pay any attention to the gossip of the other women. I was content to just stay to myself and talk to Red.

Eventually a very large, sturdy black woman, most likely in her late twenties or possibly early thirties, was assigned to Pamela's empty bunk later that afternoon. Her short black hair was matted down and dreadfully out of control. That lice shampoo was really not kind or flattering to anyone's hair. After setting up her area, she sat on the edge of the bed, humming some gospel music, and attempted to comb through her hair, separating it out into several little pigtails with little elastic bands around them. They didn't look like the elastic from socks, so I assumed she had somehow managed to smuggle them in without anyone paying attention.

Within a short while it was time for four o'clock count and the CO made her way to the new inmate's bunk.

"Jackson!"

"Yes ma'am?" she answered in a loud, boisterous but mocking voice.

The CO shook her head from side to side. "Mmm . . . mmm . . . mm. Didn't you just leave up outta here?" she asked.

"I know. What can I say? I missed y'all!" Jackson smirked as she mockingly rolled her eyes and shifted her stance in a defiant move. She appeared to be confident, strong and self-reliant. She definitely wasn't the type to make small talk or pleasant acquaintances with anyone. She seemed to know exactly what she was doing and was well aware of everything around her. It was obvious she knew some of the women in the area and eventually made her way to their bunks after count. I kept thinking she would be caught out of place, but no one seemed to question her about anything. I watched with curiosity as this woman who was apparently very "prison smart," brazenly made her way up and down the aisles after count.

Mattie was gone now, but I overheard Chopper telling others it was "her"- it was *Peaches*. By now my curiosity had gotten the best of me, and I wanted to know why everyone seemed to dread this woman who would now be sleeping in a bunk 24-inches away from me.

I didn't know the new girl who was directly below me now, except that her name was Charity and she told me she was in for ten days because she hadn't paid her child support. A tall skinny, blue-eyed blonde I knew had most likely been a beautiful young woman at one time; now conveyed a harsh, very thin and tired face. I assumed she must have been warned several times regarding the child support, or there were other extenuating circumstances for her to be sent to the state reformatory. I was pretty sure she didn't know anything about this "Peaches" woman of curiosity.

I made my way across the aisle to Patty, a very tall and heavy, but extremely pretty and quiet black girl. Most likely in her early twenties, Patty had been in Admissions about as long as I had, but never really talked to anyone.

"Hey Patty. What are you doing?"

"Nothing really. I ordered some burgers and fries from Burger King. Just waiting on them to come in." We both laughed. She had a reserved, but quirky personality.

"So, do you know who this 'Peaches' woman is that came in tonight?" I asked.

"No, I sure don't. But from what I hear, she in for murder or somethin' like that. I guess she been here before for a long time. She got out in April and now she back in again." That was the most I had ever heard Patty say about anything.

"Crap. I'm not crazy about her sleeping right next to me. I sure wish I could get out of here. My time's up. But now it will be at least another week. Well, I guess you and I had just better pray for a lot of protection!" We talked for a few more minutes before I made my way back to my top bunk before dinner time.

Red and I stayed in the atrium area after dinner that night just hanging out and talking. She didn't know anything about Peaches either, but I explained what Patty had told me. Eventually we went to our bunks and said good night. I climbed up on my bed to spend some time reading my Bible. I had really started to understand a little more about the stories and lessons of Jesus. I was still confused about a lot of things, but I was eager and curious to find out. I attended as many of the Bible studies that I could, and went to church services every Sunday night. Realizing I wanted to know more and more about the love, hope and grace of God, I prayed for true understanding and knowledge of His promises.

Be Not Afraid

"Only do not rebel against the Lord. And do not be afraid of the people of the land, because we will devour them. Their protection is gone, but the Lord is with us. Do not be afraid of them."

Numbers 14:9

Just as I turned over on my side and pulled the army blanket up over my shoulder, Peaches and a large group of her entourage approached the end of my bunk singing exceptionally loud, and extremely off-key offensive rap songs. It was certainly a shakeup of her previous soft gospel music. I tried to tune them out as I continued to read. All of a sudden Peaches grabbed a hold of both sides of the rails at the end of my bunk, and started shaking it violently. "Get up! Get up!" she screamed at me. I sat straight up like a bolt of lightning.

"What?! What do you want?" I shouted back at her.

"I said get up!" she snapped.

"Why? I'm reading and I don't want to" I angrily remarked, although a little skittish of my tone with her. I lay back down, turned on my side away from the group, covered up again, and tried to continue reading. Holding tightly onto my Bible and already frightened, I became even more troubled when Peaches walked around the other side of my bunk – the side she was not permitted to be on – and stood with her face right in front of mine.

"What's the matter with you? You don't like to sing? You too good to sing with us?" she insisted.

"Look, I just don't want to and I don't have to. Why does it matter? Now leave me alone." I was in total disbelief now that I had stood up to her. I knew I didn't want to fight her, but I couldn't back down.

She looked at me with a surprised expression, and then backed away with an angered, but confused look.

"Oh . . . ok, girl, ok . . . that how it gonna be?" she touted sarcastically. "Ok, we'll see. We'll see," as she slowly backed away from my bed, never taking her eyes off of me.

Oh great. Now I did it. What was I thinking? This was the first time I had seriously felt threatened in any way, and now realized I had snapped into my "defense" mode.

I had always been a verbal "fighter" - anytime I felt bullied or placed in any kind of hostile situation. After several years of abuse, my internal instinct was always to fight back. Although it never got me anywhere except into more trouble or more pain; I would fight and kick and scream none-the-less when I felt I had been wronged. I just couldn't seem to understand when to stop or shut up. I continued to lay awake, unable to sleep at all until much later into the night, when the welcome sound of her loud snoring soon gave me some peace of mind.

I would soon come to realize this would not be the only encounter I would endure with Peaches. Careful not to appear to be rude or indignant in any way, I would subtlety turn away from her so I wouldn't have to look at or acknowledge her. Regardless, it appeared that she had forgotten about me for the time being, and had become pre-occupied with a new project for the moment.

Almost every day Peaches made her way to the Infirmary on the prison grounds outside of the Admissions area. It was state law that if an inmate should express or indicate suffering from any form of illness or pain what-so-ever, that inmate would be required to go to the Infirmary to see a doctor, nurse or other medical personnel. It appeared that Peaches suffered from a multitude of ailments, including: back pain, ear-aches, toothaches and headaches among other things. Every day when she came back, which was always right before 4:00pm *count,* she would open up her large blue, overstuffed coat and literally dump every kind of contraband into her lockbox. Loaded down with lighters, soda pop, cigarettes, snacks and a myriad of items from the commissary, she would then make these items available to the other ladies. Only I was not certain how or what these inmates would be obligated to "pay" for the commodities.

In addition, as she made her way out and about to the Infirmary, she was not required to attend any of the mandatory classes or do any of the workload assigned to her that day. It was very obvious that Peaches knew all the "ins" and "outs" of prison life, and she not only played the system, but pretty much "ran" that place. All the women were intimidated by her and afraid of her fury if they didn't do or say exactly what she ordered them to do. I just stayed to myself and never said a word about her or what she was doing to anyone. I secretly and desperately prayed each day that she would soon be caught and taken to the "hole" (isolation). My only goal was to get out of Admissions - as quickly and safely as possible.

Cold Impressions

The next few days continued to be incredibly cold outside on the yard. I usually walked the walk-jog twice a day to keep pace with attempting to get some exercise and restore my sanity. But this day I stayed huddled by the door talking to Red for a short time before giving in to the bitter cold and going back inside. That soon proved to be a huge mistake.

As we walked back into the dorm area, the CO cornered several of us to solicit help with pushing the large laundry bins up to the laundry facility. No one responded and turned away as if she wasn't even there. "I ain't playin'. Some of you had better step up or I'll volunteer for you!" she adamantly demanded.

"What? Those things are huge and heavy!" several resisted.

"You trippin'! I ain't doing that!" another shouted out.

At the distinct disadvantage of being located close to the CO's podium, I tried to avoid eye contact as she looked straight at me. "Come on Friend, get up here." Yep, she had my number. She knew I was always cooperative and didn't fight the system. I glanced back at Red as if to say *"If I gotta do this, so do you!"*

Begrudgingly, she stepped up beside me, however. "You owe me girl!" she stammered out. The CO selected a few others and informed us to dress warm; it would be a long and cold walk up the hill to laundry detail.

Not even possessing warm clothing, let alone gloves, hats or boots, I dreaded going back out into the bitter winter air. Some of the other women taunted us as we began loading and pushing the large clothes bins up to the exit area.

"You all stupid! You think you get extra points or somethin' for doin' they dirty work? *Shoot* . . . you don't get nothin' for kissin' their *a. .es!*"

"Why you let them do you like that? You stupid!" another touted.

The thought never even occurred to me that we would have a choice. . . and I'm quite sure we didn't. Just negative women talkin' more negative talk.

Escorted to the front entrance, as the alarms sounded and the doors opened; this was not at all what I had envisioned when I would finally be able to walk through those doors. Clad only in the thin worn-out jumpsuit, a lightweight pair of socks, tennis shoes and heavy coat, I tried desperately to keep the hood around my face as I stepped out into the harsh blustery cold. Freezing and icy winds whipping through my hair and sharp frost biting at my face, my eyes were watering and stinging from the intense cold. I could only take one heavy step at a time on the icy hill, trying desperately not to lose traction or control of the heavy bins.

"No, go to the left!" one of the women shouted. "Turn it hard!" It was nearly impossible to keep moving, but we had no choice. The air in my lungs burning, it was very difficult to breathe. After what seemed like an eternity, we eventually reached the huge brick laundry building. Pushing the cart up onto the loading dock and inside the loading area, the brief few moments of warm air gave some immediate relief to my lungs and frozen skin.

As we turned to leave, "Whoa! Where you think y'all going? You're not done yet! You still have to unload and put these in the proper shoots!" The sergeant that *greeted* us at the entrance area was a hard-core, large white woman with gray-streaked long hair, wrapped on top of her head in a bun. Shouting instructions and obscenities to us, her demeanor was harsh and crude. But I was okay with that; the warm air was a welcome blessing. Eventually we emptied the laundry bin and were instructed to take the empty clothes container back with us. Trying frantically not to fall in my slippery tennis shoes, we all but ran down the hill to the Admissions building. I never dreamt I would actually want to go back inside that building again.

Satan's Playground

By the end of the week, I had somehow managed to steer clear of any further confrontations with Peaches. It was Friday afternoon and 4:00pm count time. Everyone was situated on the end of their beds as required, except Peaches. Unless you were at your assigned work area, at the Infirmary under a doctor's order, or other pre-excused and confirmed status of absence, you were considered "out-of-place" and/or AWOL. This could be reason to assume you had possibly escaped or were in some other type of unauthorized situation.

The minutes continued to tick by. The sergeant was called to the barracks. The CO resumed with the remaining count. I could only hold my breath with the anticipation and excitement of the thought that Peaches had finally been caught with all of her smuggled goods, and immediately escorted to isolation. *"Oh God, thank you! I KNOW you hear my prayers."*

Just as I opened my eyes with final relief, Peaches was standing at the foot of my bunk. "You thought I wasn't coming back, didn't you?" she quietly asked. "In fact, you were hoping I would never come back," her dark eyes piercing my heart.

I could only stare back at her in total disbelief and silence. *"How did she know that? What was within this woman that she predicted my every thought?"* I was beginning to realize more than ever before that this truly was Satan's playground. . . that he walked the corridors of the dorm with no fear of ever being stopped.

Although I couldn't realize it at the time, God *was* answering my prayers. I had asked for knowledge - for truth about who He was. He was showing me clearly that evil has no shame, no boundaries, nor dread of destruction - and that Satan was real and alive. He walks this earth, lying and destroying everything and everyone in his path.

God wanted me to realize - ***to conceive vividly as real; to be fully aware of; to bring into concrete existence*** - for how could I otherwise truly understand or desire hope, protection, or the grace of God if I didn't understand and believe that evil is real?

The Lion's Den

"How long, Lord? Will you forget me forever?" David lamented. *"How long must I wrestle with my thoughts and day after day have sorrow in my heart? How long will my enemy triumph over me?"*

Psalm 13:1–2

It was yet another week that I didn't hear my name called for transportation. Tuesday morning and going on six weeks now, I was becoming more anxious and fearful. Why weren't they calling me to leave? Several others had come and gone before me. They called Red's name that morning. She didn't know if she would be going back to her county jail or into general population. We had already exchanged phone numbers, but my heart sank as I realized I might not ever see her again. She was truly my saving grace - the only one to honestly be at my side for every sad, scary, funny, weird and crazy moment. I hugged her and told her I would never forget her. I realized she had been the angel God sent to me in this huge hole of darkness and forbidden territory.

Shocked with the realization that I had managed to steer clear from the rage of Peaches, and many others throughout the week, I could only question how much longer could I be expected to survive this place of sheer madness? Every day was a challenge of dealing with women who were crying, homesick, severely depressed and suicidal. Others were yelling obscenities, threatening, and physically fighting with each other. Women struggling and screaming with the pains of withdrawal, and whistles screeching as some were caught smoking, having sex, or smearing feces on the bathroom walls. *"Oh, please God, please get me out of here."*

Now early Friday morning of that same week, it was Peaches' turn to sweep and mop the floors around us before 5:00am inspection. We were all expected to take turns, but Peaches never did. I wasn't going to question it. Charity and the other newbie atop Peaches' bunk said they weren't going to mop the floor – it wasn't their turn, and to just forget it. With a heavy sigh, I crawled out of bed and crossed the atrium to get the mop and broom out of the closet. I really didn't feel very good that morning, but began cleaning; attempting to be quiet and not wake Peaches up. I was almost done when I accidently bumped the handle of the mop on the edge of her bed causing her to wake up. Bolting straight up, "What are you doing you *scanky bi . . .?!"* she screamed at me.

I kept saying I was sorry but she continued to call me everything but a white woman - although actually she did tell me to get my "ashy white a. ." out of her face! That was the end all. I had been holding my inner peace far too long.

However, I was shocked when I instantly turned and said "Look! I'm not in your ugly face and I'm tired of doing all of your work!" Was that me? Did those words just come out of my mouth? What part did I not understand to keep my mouth shut?

Peaches immediately jumped up out of bed and towered over me, screaming and pushing her index finger into my chest. "You don't know who you talkin' to girl! You think you playin' with me? It's on now! You better be lookin' out behind you *bi…!!"*

"Oh, my dearest Jesus . . . if you have ever heard any prayer I've ever said, please listen to me now. I need out of here! I need you to protect me," I frantically whispered to myself. I was horribly and totally terrified. I immediately left and went to the atrium area, returned the mop to the closet, and sat in the metal chairs in front of the CO's desk until count was called. I was shaking in absolute fear.

I sat there in silence and remembered thinking about watching a late night black and white movie with my mom when I was a little girl. I didn't remember the name of the movie, but wondered if this was how the Christians felt when they were thrown in the den with the lions. The only relief I had was that I did remember that the lions didn't kill them. Then I realized it - maybe I really was a *Christian* and God was protecting me. Could that be possible?

That same afternoon, I lay on my bunk thinking back through the episode of that morning. Why do I have this instantaneous reaction to be so righteous and fight back? But then I recalled recently reading a story from the Bible that had portrayed the anger of Jesus at times. He had entered the temple courts and once he saw what was taking place there, He could hold His peace no longer. He drove out all who were buying and selling there. He overturned the tables of the money collectors and the benches of those selling their merchandise. He had had enough! They were disgracing, stealing and using the temple, the house of prayer, as a "den for robbers."

12 Jesus entered the temple courts and drove out all who were buying and selling there. He overturned the tables of the money changers and the benches of those selling doves. 13 "It is written," he said to them, "'My house will be called a house of prayer,¹ but you are making it 'a den of robbers.'"

Matthew 21:12-13

Slowly but surely, I was becoming aware God was using these situations to teach me; to show me things through His eyes that I had never seen before. I had been that robber, that disgraceful person who stole and lied to others who had trusted me. Now it was up to me to realize the error and sin of my ways.

Over and over again, I had asked God to please forgive me and to teach me His ways. I knew that although God had never "condemned" me to prison, He had "allowed" me to be sentenced because I had to experience the pain, the fear, the deceit of the world to know how to fight against it. I had to learn how to be able to discern the truth from the lies of the *evil one*. How many times in my life had I believed those brazen and audacious lies?

Mistaken Identity

I continued to desperately pray for answers, because I couldn't see any way out of this. I knew that I knew that Peaches would make good on her word. Sure enough, she stood at the end of my bunk that same day and calmly said "Hey Friend. CO wants to see you."

I sat up and calmly asked "For what?"

"Oh, you're not in any trouble or anything. Really, you're not. She just wants to ask you about somethin'" she explained, just as cool and as nice as could possibly be. "Come on, I'll go with you. It'll be ok," as she smiled at me. There was no question. Now I knew something was up.

I cautiously climbed down off the bed, looking around me at all times, fearful of a trap that might be set for me. I hesitantly walked past the open bathroom doors and then quickly out onto the atrium area. "See I told you it was going to be ok," she smiled again.

As we approached the large wooden desk, the CO stood up and asked me very sternly "Do you have illegal contraband in your lockbox that I need to be aware of?"

I immediately and precariously looked at Peaches who stood there with a smirk on her face. "No mam'" I adamantly denied - never taking my eyes off of Peaches.

"It's my understanding that you have lighters, cigarettes and other illegal items in your possession," the CO continued. Realizing that Peaches had obviously reported this information to the CO, I became more terrified as I recalled the previous incident of someone filling my lockbox with contraband items. But that made no sense. I had a lock on it now. Would it be possible that she was able to break into my box somehow?

"No mam'. I don't even smoke. I would never take or hold any illegal items for anyone," I quickly stammered out . . . and yet realizing all of this coming from a convicted thief?

"Well, I guess we need to go take a look, then don't we?" the CO declared.

As she stepped out from behind the desk and walked in front of us, I quickly turned to Peaches and quietly mouthed "What did you do? You KNOW I don't have anything in that box, and there better not be anything or I'm taking you down with me!"

Now about ten steps behind the CO, Peaches instantly became enraged, turned her head and threatened to spit in my face (an immediate misdemeanor charge of assault, and most definitely immediate transport to isolation) if I said anything. "CO!" I shouted out as I ran ahead. "She just threatened me! She said she was going to spit on me if I said anything else!"

Oh, Lord. Now sounding like a spoiled rotten kid telling on their siblings – *"Mommy! She looked at me!"* I felt somewhat foolish and ridiculous. And yet - I would fight her. I could not allow this outright bullying from anyone ever again. But the look of shock on her face was . . . well - priceless!

Stopping in her tracks and emphatically turning around to face us, "What's going on here?" the CO firmly demanded.

Immediately Peaches spoke up "Oh, you know what? I was mistaken. It wasn't her at all! It was some other white girl. They all look alike to me!" she blurted out.

"Really? That's the best you can come up with?" was all I could think. But yet I knew that *she knew;* I wasn't backing down from her.

"Look, I don't have time for this ridiculous nonsense! Now you better get your story straight Jackson! Do you know for a fact that someone has illegal items in their possession or not?" she insisted.

"Oh yes, yes, I do. Here I'll take you to her," she quickly responded.

"Let's go Jackson!" and then she turned toward me "You're dismissed Friend."

Once again in total disbelief, I slowly walked behind them and watched as Peaches walked up and down the aisle between the bunks. I was curious as to what she would do next, and who she would point the finger at.

She eventually stopped at Patty's bed, the large black girl across from my bunk. I stood there in total confusion as I was pretty sure Patty didn't look anything at all like me - or any other white woman in there. I was also in shock as she accused this poor girl of holding illegal items. I really didn't know if Patty did have anything, and wondered if that was why Peaches had called her out. Or was it because Patty and I had been hanging out with each other recently? I prayed not.

The CO looked through Patty's box but didn't find anything. After several other "mistaken identities", Peaches finally pointed out a young white girl with long blond hair who was holding several items. I believe the CO was becoming very angry, and Peaches finally had to point the finger at one of her own regular clientele.

It was lunch time and as everyone took their place in line in the hallway, the accused girl was escorted to the Sergeant's office. Peaches followed directly behind them and as she passed by, she glared at me to let me know it wasn't over. I quickly looked at Patty to see if she saw her evil look. Patty just shook her head in disbelief.

After lunch, I climbed back up on my bunk, only to fear what would come next. And yet, I praised and thanked God for His divine protection of me once again. I began to truly understand and realize that God was real - not only for my cousins or "other" Christians; but for me - a sinner, a liar, a criminal.

The Bus Stops Here

"You will not have to fight this battle. Take up your positions; stand firm and see the deliverance the LORD will give you. . . Do not be afraid; do not be discouraged. Go out to face them tomorrow, and the LORD will be with you."

2 Chronicles 20:17

Somehow, I got through yet another week-end without any additional incidents, but I felt as if Peaches was only biding her time. What was she waiting for? I didn't know what could possibly be going through her mind, and yet each day that passed without confrontation was another day of blessing.

Finally, it was Monday night. I could barely sleep with the anticipation of leaving the next morning. Once again, I had made certain to get my things gathered up and ready to go just as soon as my name was called. At long last 4:00am lights came up to get ready for the day. My heart was beating with anticipation of finally being able to leave. I just knew that today would be the day I would depart on the "bus". I scurried to the bathroom to wash my face, brush my teeth and run a comb through my hair. I quickly swept the floor around me and made my bed. I didn't care if the floor was mopped, or if Peaches yelled obscenities, or anything else that could possibly happen to ruin my day - it wouldn't be possible. Nothing would take away my joy of getting on the bus that morning.

I lined up for breakfast and thought the dry toast and chalky orange drink tasted especially good that morning. Afterward I walked back to the dorm with Patty. We were both expecting to *ride out* that day. We wished each other good luck and went to our bunks waiting for mail and transportation calls.

Almost 7:30am, the sun came up that early Tuesday morning. *"Thank you, God. Thank you for safely bringing me through this time of turmoil and sparing me any more problems."* I was so very grateful and relieved. I sensed God's presence and felt warm and safe again. I don't remember that I had received any mail that day, but no matter. Just the thought of leaving was sufficient good news for me. I lay on my bunk and awaited transport call. Very soon thereafter the call was made.

"Listen up! If your name and number is called, gather your things immediately and report to the CO's desk for transportation!" the CO loudly proclaimed. This was it! My belongings in hand, I stood at the end of my bunk awaiting the sound of my name and state number to be announced. Becoming quite anxious, I continued to listen for several more minutes.

Then the list of those transporting out that morning was repeated. In total disbelief, I was numb and sick to my stomach with the devastating awareness that my name was not on that list. How could this be true? It had been 37 days. Certainly, there must be some mistake. How could so many others go out before me? Damn pregnant girls.

"I don't understand God. Why? Why am I having to stay in this place of fear and terror? I thought you were protecting me?" I felt betrayed and that God had certainly forgotten about me. I had been faithfully praying, seeking and thanking Him. I had believed that He heard me, but why was He not answering me? I truly didn't believe I could make it another whole week in this horrific situation.

In total defeat, I crawled back up on my bunk and wrapped up in the hard, course blanket. I turned on my side and curled up as small as I could to somehow feel safe, even if just for a few moments. But I couldn't get over the feeling that God had abandoned me in my time of need. Maybe I had been right all along. Maybe He really wasn't there at all for me like He was for other people. After all, how could He have allowed all of the dreadful and unspeakable things in my whole life to ever happen to me? There would be no place for me to turn now. I would just have to stand on my own as I always had, counting on my own thoughts and perception. It was what I had always done anyhow - obviously not very well, but it was what I was familiar with.

The Burning Bed

[18] You have not come to a mountain that can be touched and that is burning with fire; to darkness, gloom and storm; . . . [22] But you have come to Mount Zion, to the city of the living God, the

89

heavenly Jerusalem. You have come to thousands upon thousands of angels in joyful assembly, [23] to the church of the firstborn, whose names are written in heaven. You have come to God, the Judge of all, to the spirits of the righteous made perfect, [24] to Jesus the mediator of a new covenant . . ."

Hebrews 12:18;22-24

Patty's name was not called either. We were both crushed when we realized we would not be leaving for yet another week. It would be seven days now before we could possibly be transferred out. I realized I could not count on anything or anyone in this place any longer. I recalled my very first day when Mattie had told me *"You forget where you are girl!"* That was the hard-core truth. You are completely under the rule and power of everyone there. You cannot make decisions, nor have any rights. You have lost all freedom of even the most insignificant things. You are told when to eat, when to sleep, when permitted to go to the bathroom, or when you can shower. I felt powerless and out of control of my own life and destiny. At that moment I didn't want to read or believe anything else about the hope or promises of God.

That afternoon I attended yet another required class and listened to a fairly young woman, possibly in her thirties, give her testimony regarding her many years as an alcoholic. She shared that while she was under the influence, she had committed several serious crimes, including stabbing someone with a knife during the robbery of a convenience store. She had been sentenced to a total of fifteen years, and it had now been six years. I couldn't even imagine. My heart ached for her. I sensed that possibly I was supposed to hear her story so I could realize I really didn't have it so bad; but yet I failed to feel any sense of relief at that moment. Even as she explained how she had changed and had hope for the future, I couldn't relate to her story right now. I had spiraled down that deep dark hole of fear and depression. My heart had hardened and become cold with trepidation and fear.

After dinner, I didn't go to library or Bible class that Tuesday evening. I just lay on my bunk, curled up and tried to shut the world out. By now the loud talking, singing, crying and fighting of the other inmates was of no substantial concern to me. I just stayed to myself and didn't want to talk to anyone. There would be no consoling of my heart or mind that evening, and my fear just kept escalating with thoughts of another whole week with Peaches sleeping just two feet away from me. How could I possibly escape her malicious oppression?

Drawing near to time for lights out, my deepest fears became reality. I could feel the presence of someone just inches from my face. I opened my eyes to see Peaches had placed her chin squarely on the bed rail, her dark eyes starring coldly and directly into my own eyes. I couldn't move, my body frozen with terror and unbearable fright. "Ever smelt the stench of flesh burning, Friend? You think you some *fu. . . . harda. .,* or somethin'?"

Terrified by her words, I recalled a story that she had set one of the CO's on fire on a previous stint she had served.

Everyone swore up and down it was the God-honest truth. "You better not think 'bout sleeping tonight Friend, 'cause I'm gonna light you up *bi. . . .!* I in here for murder; you think I care what happens to you? And you think you gonna go out there and be safe on the grounds? 'Cause my girlfriend in here for murder too, and we got you *set* girl!" She coldly and brazenly winked at me and walked away.

I couldn't breathe. I literally felt like the wind had been knocked out of me. I slowly sat up and looked around. Had anyone seen her threaten me? Did anyone at all hear what just happened? I didn't know who I could trust or what to do. Literally paralyzed with fear, I could only sit on the edge of the bed. *"God please, please help me"* I prayed in desperation. Realizing I had turned away from God that very morning, had He given up on me and left me for dead now? Could He somehow find it in His heart to forgive me and protect me now? *"I'm sorry, God. I'm so sorry. Please, please forgive me and save me. What do I do? Please don't leave me. I need you."*

I was physically sick to my stomach and shaking all over. Should I go to the CO and report what just happened? What if word got out that I was a snitch and it would be worse for me? But then, what could be worse than being set on fire? Confused, scared and broken, I vowed to stay awake all night. But I knew I couldn't stay awake for an entire week. And then what? Would I go to general population on the grounds and be under the constant fear of her girlfriend, or any of her "gang," only to anticipate the day Peaches would finally be released to population?

I lay awake for hours, never moving, always on my side facing her with my eyes wide open. She eventually fell fast asleep, but I feared she might awaken and I wouldn't hear her sneak up on me in my sleep.

After what seemed like an eternity, I slowly turned to look at the clock above the CO's podium. I could see it was 3:36am; lights would come up in about 20 minutes. My eyelids growing heavy, I only needed to close them for a few moments of relief. Then, in what seemed to be only seconds, the loud clicking sound and bright lights turning up alarmed me it was time to start the day.

Sensing a huge sigh of relief deep within, I didn't get up right away. I didn't need to clean, and I would dress quickly before 5:00am inspection. I knew Peaches *never ever* got up until the absolute last minute before count. I tried to steal a few more minutes of rest, never really falling asleep, and joyfully listening to all of the loud, obnoxious chatter, moaning & groaning around me. Although so thankful I had somehow escaped the terror of the night, I knew I wasn't completely safe; and if I were to fall into a deep slumber, it would only take a second for the flicker of a lighter to catch my bed on fire.

The Warning

"*[1] Whoever dwells in the shelter of the Most High will rest in the shadow of the Almighty. [2] I will say of the LORD, "He is my refuge and my fortress, my God, in whom I trust." [3] Surely he will save you from the fowler's snare and from the deadly pestilence... [5] You will not fear the terror of night, nor the arrow that flies by day, [6] nor the pestilence that stalks in the darkness, nor the plague that destroys at midday."*

Psalm 91, 1-3; 5,6

Numb to everything around me, I slowly walked to breakfast with Patty. Under my breath, I quietly asked her "Did you see or hear what Peaches said to me last night before lights out?"

"No, what happened?" she inquired. After I explained everything in detail, her face displayed her own fearful shock. She quickly warned me "Girl, you better get to the CO and ask to be put in the hole for real!"

"Why would I want to be put in the 'hole'?" I replied.

"At least you in protective custody! *Shoot*... don't let that *bi*... kill your *a*..! And you know she will too!" she exclaimed.

I had heard rumors that the "hole" was not a pleasant or tolerable place to be. You were stripped of all clothing except a large white canvas sack dress, and placed in solitary

93

confinement. A plate of "leftovers" all tossed together would be pushed through the door slot to you for your meals. You were only permitted to come out into a secluded area once a day for one hour. No phone calls, no reading, no programs, no contact with anyone what-so-ever. I recalled my very first day driving down the long gravel driveway and thinking at least they couldn't kill me in here. I would now understand that was *not* the truth. You are never safe from the snares or entrapment of Satan.

After breakfast I asked Patty to please stay close and go out to the yard with me. It bothered me that I was now placing this very large, but very sweet girl in her own position of danger to be associated with me; but she didn't even hesitate. I needed someone to watch over and protect me; and I desperately needed to get out of the same area as Peaches to think about what to do.

Not quite as cold with the sun out on this otherwise gloomy day, we walked the path for a little while, never leaving the sight of the CO's on yard duty. "Girl, I'm tellin' you, you better get to the CO right now. You don't know what she capable of." I knew Patty was right, I just didn't want to do anything to jeopardize my chances of leaving anytime soon. I wanted assurance I could still leave at my designated time.

"I pray to God, Patty, that I'll be able to go to the Pre-Release Center. I can't stay here. I know I'm not safe anywhere on this compound."

As the CO's announced time to clear the yard, we made our way back to the entrance of the dorm. Suddenly several of the other inmates came up and warned me, "Peaches out to get you girl! You better watch your back. She ain't playin'!"

"You not safe here, Friend. She got the word out for you. You better get to that hole!" Several others chimed in their words of warning and concern for me.

It was confirmed. I boldly stepped inside the door and headed straight to the center of the atrium for the CO's desk. Determined that I would not perish in this atrocious place, I marched fearlessly across the cold gray linoleum floor. Just as I reached approximately half-way distance to the desk, the CO shouted "Listen up! If I call your name, come directly to the CO's desk!" Confused, I stopped dead in my tracks. What was this about? I listened intently as she began the list of names.

And He Shall Call Me by Name

"Lift up your eyes and look to the heavens: Who created all these? He who brings out the starry host one by one and calls forth each of them by name. Because of His great power and mighty strength, not one of them is missing."

Isaiah 40:26

Obviously alphabetically, the CO soon called out "Friend, Nanette!" I had no idea what this could possibly mean, but I quickly stepped up to the duck-tape line securely placed across the floor in front of the desk. Not permitted to cross this make-shift line, I was elated that Patty's name was also called, and she rushed to take her place beside me. We both looked at each other with an inquisitive look and half-smile, and shrugged our shoulders with disbelief. As we stood there waiting for additional instructions with approximately twenty other women, all of the remaining inmates were instructed to return to their bunks for lock-down.

The CO continued, "If I have called your name, you are to go immediately to your area, gather up all of your belongings and return to this area. Do *not* stop to talk to anyone, do *not* cause any delay, and do not run. You have five minutes to return to this area where you will be given further instructions and ID verification."

I immediately turned on my heels and walked as quickly as possible to my bunk to retrieve my personal items and clothing from the lock box. Now lying on her bed just inches away, Peaches sat up and sarcastically smirked at me, "So you think you safe now, huh Friend? You think you got away from me? Nope! I know right where you are, and you goin' down *bi. . . !*" Although frightened by her further threats, I didn't answer or look at her. I proceeded to frantically stuff everything that was in my lock box into the white mesh laundry bag, and scurried out of the dorm. I never looked back; I just kept a firm pace to the atrium.

Within a few minutes, everyone had returned to the assigned area. Count and identification were immediately taken, and then instructions to proceed to the dining area located near the outside door. I couldn't understand or believe it. Was I honestly on my way out of the Admissions area? I didn't know where I was going, but right then I didn't care.

"Oh, thank you God, thank you Jesus, thank you most wonderful Holy Spirit. I know I don't deserve this, but once again you have given me favor, grace and protection," I whispered to myself.

"Have I not commanded you? Be strong and courageous. Do not be afraid; do not be discouraged, for the LORD your God will be with you wherever you go."

Joshua 1:9

CHAPTER 7

❧ *Preservation* ❧

n: The act, process, or result of preserving something such as the activity or process of keeping something valued alive, intact, or free from damage, decay, or destruction. The act or activity of keeping something in an existing and usually satisfactory condition. Protection, safeguarding, upholding, maintenance, salvation.

"Though I walk in the midst of trouble, you preserve my life. You stretch out your hand against the anger of my foes; with your right hand you save me."

Psalm 138:7

The day before Thanksgiving, and now into 38 days of confinement; I remained in my seat in the lunchroom until they called my name. Some of the ladies had already been called and were being escorted to "discharge." From there they would be transferred outside of the penitentiary walls. Patty was one of those women. Ordered not to speak to anyone, I gave her a quick nod and smile of *"good luck."* Apprehensive that I would remain on the compound, I could only thank God that at least I was being transported out of the Admissions area and away from harm at this moment. For the first time in weeks I felt I could breathe a small sense of relief. God had answered my prayers of safety and deliverance from the snares of the evil within these walls. He had rescued me from almost certain death. But I also knew I would still have to be on high alert from those around me in "general population." I would have no way of knowing who may be a part of Peaches' group of committed followers. I wouldn't be able to trust anyone.

Eventually assigned to one of the trustees waiting to escort us to our destination, I joined the other five or six women in my group who would be going to the same location. Wrapped up in my coat and clutching my bag of minimal belongings, I stepped out into the cold air. The trustee immediately explained that we had been assigned to Hale Cottage. She stated this was minimum security, and we would be afforded a lot more privileges. She went on to explain, "Oh, you still in prison girl. But you have the freedom to move about the compound and have access to more activities, jobs and free time."

She continued to further describe and point out the locations of the library, church, beauty salon, cafeteria, commissary, campus college, computer lab; and a myriad of other facilities we would have access to. I hesitantly asked, "You mean we can just go to these places on our own?"

"You have to sign out on your own time, when you're not at work, or other mandatory assignments. But yes, you can visit these locations," she clarified.

Not certain that was a safe thing to do, I quietly wondered to myself, "*Where was the maximum-security building?*" My only thought was that Peaches or her girlfriend - or anyone of their band of constituents, could somehow still get a hold of me. "*Ok God, just one day at a time. Please find it in your heart to continue to protect me. I would have rather been transported outside these walls to the Pre-Release Center, but I'll trust you.*" At that point, I had no choice but to trust Him. One last question for the trustee: "Why are we going out on a Wednesday?"

"I'm not sure, but I heard something about too many *"pregos"* (pregnant women) holding everybody up, so they had to move you out somewhere else for now."

"For now?" someone else asked. "Yeah, you probably been placed here until they know for sure where you goin'" she answered. *"Oh, thank you pregnant ladies!"* I humbly thought to myself.

My heart was filled with hope once again. Maybe I still had a chance to go to the Pre-Release Center.

In the Midst of It All

"¹And now, brothers and sisters, we want you to know about the grace that God has given . . . ² In the midst of a very severe trial, their overflowing joy and their extreme poverty welled up in rich generosity."

2 Corinthians 8:1-2

We soon reached the cottage and were escorted inside to the CO's desk, located just inside the door of a fairly small room. Several metal folding chairs were placed in neat rows in front of the desk. An inmate was standing on one side of the room at an ironing board, ironing her clothes while watching a television located on the wall; and another was popping popcorn in a microwave. Instructed to take a seat on one of the chairs, I was stunned as I observed that everyone just seemed to be roaming about. Women were going in and out the door (after signing in/out), as well as having access to an iron, a TV and a microwave? I was confused, but very grateful for such luxuries. This appeared to be a "hidden treasure" within an otherwise gloomy and hopeless living situation.

Eventually we were processed in, assigned our bunks, provided with clean bed rolls and *pillows;* and then escorted into a very large dorm area. It appeared to be a room filled with approximately 300 beds, and I could only pray I would be assigned a bed fairly close to the CO's podium again. Stopping at a bunk and glancing down at her clipboard, the CO announced "Friend . . . number?" I rattled off my now well-memorized inmate number. "Top bunk" she announced before moving on to the next area.

This time I was only about eight beds from the CO's area, and that was ok. I could live with that - literally. I was also in utter disbelief that this bed had a ladder. I was beyond pleased and very grateful. Although by now I had lost approximately fifteen pounds, and had pretty much mastered the art of climbing on the top bunk; I was still appreciative that I would not be hitting my shins on the bed rails any longer. I threw my bedroll on the bunk and asked my *roomie* to the left which lock-box was mine. After pointing out the correct box, she revealed her name to be Amnesty.

Humm . . . what an unusual name; or possibly just an irony on words to be named that with a definition of "pardon of conviction, freedom, mercy". A beautiful name; only praying her name would someday hold true to its meaning for her. But then again, I had to think about the true meaning of "Peaches: 'One resembling a peach; as in sweetness, beauty, or excellence. Sweet, savory, delicious fruit seeded with a hard-central stone". Appropriate. That was a prayer I would have to totally give to God.

"But I tell you, love your enemies and pray for those who persecute you."

Matthew 5:44

Unloading my belongings into the box and securing the lock, I looked about the room. Standing at the end of my bunk, I searched up and down the aisles to see if I could spot a kind, familiar face. But then I surmised "*What could be the possibility of that ever happening?*"

A majority of the bunks were empty, and Amnesty explained most of the women were at work, school or other locations on campus. I was still in awe of the leniency of this dorm. I continued to ask questions about the shower schedule, phone privileges, and other *need-to know* information. I was surprised to learn you could take showers whenever you wanted, for as long as you wanted; and once available to me, I could actually have a razor to shave my legs! I would also have access to the phones anytime between 7:00am and 11:00pm, at which time the phones would be shut off. Commissary was on Fridays, and I would have to put my order in today to receive anything by then. I didn't have much money on my "*books,*" but I would look to see how much razors and body wash would be. Maybe I would even have enough for baby powder or deodorant. I just wanted to feel clean again.

After making my bed, I went to the CO's desk to request a commissary order and inquire about the phones. I wanted to call home and tell everyone I had been moved out of Admissions, and that I felt safe now.

I had actually never written anything to tell Don or any of my children about my horrific confrontations with Peaches, however. I didn't want to scare them any more than they already were for me. I was also excited to tell them of the privileges I now had. But I would have to wait until that evening to call as no one would be home on a Wednesday morning. I certainly didn't want to call my parents as they were still angry with me about the whole situation of Jennifer going back to the apartment to live with Don. I couldn't take any more scolding, disapproval or lectures about what a mess I had made out of everyone's life right now.

I made my way back to my area to go through the commissary list. On the way I continued to look around for a familiar face; hoping there would be someone who could help me make my way around in this new and unfamiliar territory. I also wanted desperately to be able to share my previous experiences of fear and almost fatal mishaps with Peaches, with someone I knew. Afraid to trust anyone else, I longed to be able to talk to Red.

I climbed up the ladder and made out my order. I had approximately $8 on my books. It was enough to get everything but the baby powder; I would have to get it the next time. But I did have enough to get a Snickers candy bar, and that sounded like absolute heaven to me! As I continued to read through the entire commissary now available to me, I dreamt of the many other items I would someday be able to purchase.

As I envisioned the possibilities, 10:00am count was announced. Assuming this was a standing count, I climbed down from my bunk and took my place at the end of the bed. Many of the "missing" ladies returned to their areas and took their place as well. After count, I really wasn't certain what to do as I had not yet received any assignments or meetings I would be required to attend. I decided to take advantage of the free time and take a nap. I was extremely exhausted from not having any sleep the previous night.

As I climbed back up on my bed, I peered over the top of the long stone wall between myself and the extensive row of bunks on the other side. Directly across from me on the other side of the wall, with her head facing away from me; I noticed a woman lying on her bed with one of her legs propped up on the other, while reading a book. But the most prominent thing I noticed was that she had the brightest long red hair. I hesitated as I couldn't conceivably believe it to be true; but then I questioned her, "Red, is that *you* Red?" The young woman sat up and turned to face me.

It *was* Red! We were both astounded and giddy as we simultaneously realized we had been reunited - and right across the wall from each other! We were like two junior high school girls at summer camp as we raced around the wall to see each other, and vowed to catch up on all that had taken place. I couldn't possibly imagine that in the midst of this huge campus of over 2,500 women, I would be placed in the very dorm, the very bed across from my friend. Over and over again I was seeing the hand of God blessing, protecting, and showing me His unquestionable love and mercy. I wasn't quite sure how to process all of this; I certainly didn't deserve it.

Giving Thanks

> *"I will give thanks to you, LORD, with all my heart; I will tell of all your wonderful deeds."*
>
> Psalm 9:1

"Come on. Let's go up to the library. There's too much going on in here to talk" Red suggested. We signed out and made our way to the library. It was a little warmer and sunny that day. The walk wasn't too bad at all.

"I just can't believe you're able to come and go and have everything available to you in here," I exclaimed. "And a pillow and a ladder? That's awesome!"

"Sure beats Admissions doesn't it?" Red continued. "Did they say anything to you about getting your state clothes yet?"

"No, not yet" I responded.

"Well they will soon enough."

Noticing that everyone had on khaki pants and light green shirts in our dorm; but others on the walkway wore various colored shirts, I asked "Is the color of your shirt to designate your dorm?"

"No, that's for your security clearance. You'll have green for minimum level. Blue is medium, pink is high level, and red is maximum security or "*Lifers*." White is for lockdown or the *hole*." Red explained.

"Have you ever seen any of the red shirts?" I inquired.

"Oh no, that's maximum. They have their own area and not allowed out in general population. You will never see any of them." Red assured me.

"Well, thank you Lord for that!" I announced. I then proceeded to tell Red of my fear, and what had taken place regarding Peaches while she had been gone.

"Oh my God! Are you serious? Would she have really set you on fire?" Red questioned.

"Oh, there's no doubt in my mind. I'm not sure what she was waiting for, but I'm certain she couldn't have known we would be taken out early. Look, I'm telling you the truth. I have prayed and prayed and I know that I know that God has answered my prayers and has been protecting me, Red. I don't always understand how or when He will do it, but it's real," I humbly remarked.

"Therefore, since we are surrounded by such a great cloud of witnesses, let us throw off everything that hinders, and the sin that so entangles us. And let us run with perseverance the race marked out for us."

Hebrews 12:1

We continued on to the library, where we talked and I was able to check out a few books. We then proceeded back to the cottage. Just as I arrived, the CO caught me as I was signing back in. "Friend?"

"Yes, ma'am?" I answered.

"You need to take this order over to intake and pick up your gear. You know where that is?" she asked.

"No, ma'am I don't."

Red instantly spoke up "I do. I'll take her over." We both signed back out for the intake building. After turning in my large, worn-out jumpsuit, I was pleased to be able to pick out medium size pants and a button-down shirt. I was also thankful for new socks, underwear, and daily essential needs. As I finished signing out everything that had been issued to me, Red informed "We better be getting right back. It's almost time for lunch."

We took our place in line and waited almost 20 minutes as the women made their way through "turnstile lines" in what appeared to be the largest dining hall I had ever seen. There had to be over 800 seats in the eating area. "Big, isn't it?" Red exclaimed. And three different lunch times for each level," she added. So grateful to have her with me, I followed her lead to a seat she designated. "It's better to stay on this side. Most of the troublemakers sit over in that area," she pointed out. She further explained that this was where she worked for the breakfast and evening meals.

We finished our lunch and conversation and then decided to go to back to the dorm and rest. Red would have to leave later that afternoon to return to the mess hall immediately after 4:00pm count. As we climbed on our bunks, "Do you want to go to work with me tonight?" she asked.

"Am I allowed to?" I questioned.

"Yea, I'm pretty sure. We'll check with the CO. You don't have any assignments, do you?"

"No, not yet." I quickly answered.

"Then it'll be okay. We won't get back until after 8:00pm." she remarked.

I only knew that I wanted to take a shower and call home that night, but this would help pass the time until then. "Ok, but please make sure I'm up for count. I haven't had any sleep at all." I lay down to get some much-needed rest for a few hours.

Red washed huge pots and pans while I wiped down tables and swept the floors after dinner that night. As I anxiously envisioned talking to Don and my children that evening, I couldn't help but be saddened as well. Here it was, the night before Thanksgiving, and thoughts that I would normally be baking pumpkin rolls, roasting the turkey and preparing for a large dinner with my family was very daunting.

When the kids were little, they would help make name cards for everyone, excitedly setting the table and decorating for the big day. The next morning, they would awake early to the aromatic smells of cinnamon rolls and pies baking, and watch Thanksgiving Day parades on television. My heart sank. It would be an experience I would not have this year. Instead I was cleaning the dining hall of a prison.

I didn't even know where everyone would be going for dinner this year. I knew Mom would most likely ask them, but everyone was at such odds with each other right now. I had certainly made a horrible mess out of everyone's holiday.

Wash Me of My Sins

"[1] Have mercy on me, O God, according to your unfailing love; according to your great compassion, blot out my transgressions.[2] Wash away all my iniquity and cleanse me from my sin."

Psalm 51:1-2

Defining Truth

I was anxious to get back to the dorm. I wanted to speak with Don and the kids. When Don answered the phone, he was less than receptive of my voice or good news. He told me he was very depressed and was not going anywhere for Thanksgiving dinner. When I asked what he would do, he stated "I don't know. Maybe I'll just go out to the (golf) club and get a turkey sandwich or something. I don't know what I'm doing anymore. I don't know how much longer I can take this."

Startled by his response, I really didn't know how to answer him. I could only think that as horrible as this was for me, I was trying desperately to remain positive and hopeful of the outcome. I wondered to myself how could *he* be so depressed? After all, I was the one who couldn't be home with my family. I was the one who would have to come home and face everyone, try to find a decent job, and start my new life as a convicted felon. He was still sleeping in his own bed every night. He still had a good job, and family and friends who loved him.

I was annoyed by his lack of compassion for me. But I missed him terribly, and he was the only thing that kept me going in this dreadful place. I was heartbroken. I told him I loved him, and begged him to please, please be patient with me. I asked him to please put Jennifer on the phone so I could speak with her, but he explained that she was at Jodi's right now. He went on to say that Jen would be having dinner at Jodi's house the next day. I told him again that I loved him, and goodnight; but my heart was heavy, and my hope was shattered.

I then called Jodi and Jen, Jill (my middle daughter) and Jamie (my son), each at their own homes. I told each of them how very sorry I was for everything, and how much I wished I could be there with them. Jodi assured me everything was fine, and she was making the turkey, although she had never attempted to do so before. She explained that Jill and Jamie were also helping by bringing a lot of the remaining food. But I knew deep in my heart that I had tragically let everyone down. I couldn't even begin to imagine what this was doing to any of my children or grandchildren right now. I told myself I needed to be strong, and decided not to mention anything about my episode with Peaches. I realized I had to appear to be safe, and everything good in their eyes. It was bad enough. When I hung up, I felt hopeless and alone.

I gathered up all of my things to take a shower. As I walked back through the shower area, I was consoled somewhat to know that the stalls were fairly large; and had clothing hooks, a bench and curtains in each one. Although looking all around me before stepping in, I was grateful to be away from everyone for a short while. I quickly undressed and then took my time washing and scrubbing my hair under the warm water. It felt so good and comforting.

And yet as the cleansing water ran down my body, large tears fell down my face. I sobbed as I realized once again what a horrible person I had become. I had destroyed so many lives, in so many ways. How could I ever make it up to everyone? I knew I never could. That was what was so unimaginable for me to face. I had made that dreadful decision; and now I could never take it back. I could never make things right again. I couldn't blame anyone for leaving me, or never loving or forgiving me again. Deep inside I was broken and inconsolable.

When I was done with my shower, I quickly wrapped my wet hair in a towel and pulled on a fresh clean gown. Although refreshing, I was physically exhausted and emotionally defeated. I climbed up on the bunk, pulled the blanket up over my head, and softly cried myself into a deep sleep that night.

"I am worn out from my groaning. All night long I flood my bed with weeping and drench my couch with tears."

Psalm 6:6

Turkey Day

"Don't eat the turkey! Whatever you do, don't eat the turkey! It's days old and rotten! Pass it on." Several of the women were repeating the command all the way down the line. As Red and I stood several feet back from the entrance to the dining hall, we could hear all of the commotion as many of the women sighed in disbelief.

Others were saying "Don't listen to them! They're lying. . . they only want to scare everyone and be mean."

I also overheard others proclaim this was now their 7th, 10th or 22nd year of spending Thanksgiving at the prison. I couldn't even begin to grasp that thought. I was so miserable, and this was my first year. How could anyone possibly spend so many years and holidays in a prison without children or family? Once again, I could feel that deep queasiness in the pit of my stomach of being homesick.

As we continued to make our way through the line, I watched as each plate was prepared, and shoved up on the glass counter for each inmate to grasp. Some of the women were being obnoxious and shouting to the ladies (inmates) serving the food. "Come on now! It's Thanksgiving! Put some potatoes on that plate!"

I took my plate of turkey, potatoes, gravy, green beans and a roll. I then picked up a small plate with pumpkin pie. I didn't know if the turkey really was spoiled, but it didn't look very appetizing, so I didn't eat it.

"Not goin' to eat your turkey, huh?" Red smirked.

"Nope, you can have it if you want," I laughed. "I'm not taking any chances about anything anymore. Just so glad to be here with you today," I sincerely declared.

After lunch we headed back to the dorm to rest. Although I had skipped breakfast and slept in that morning, I was still trying to catch up on my sleep.

I had agreed to help Red again that night at the dining hall. I wanted desperately to quickly pass the time away on this day. After dinner I scrubbed huge pots and pans alongside of her. The sinks were huge white, although yellowing, ceramic with brown stains. The large once-shiny yellow stone walls behind the sinks were old, faded and grimy. The uneven floors were worn-out scuffed wood, and discolored laminate, complete with holes. This had to be the original building from the turn of the century.

Red warned me to watch out for the mice and rats. "Are you serious?" I exclaimed.

"Well, I haven't actually seen any yet, but that's what I hear. This place is an old farm, you know. They're everywhere!" I quickly looked under the sink and at all the holes in the walls. I was seriously ready to go back to the dorm and climb on my top bunk!

When we finally did get back to the cottage that night, I was very leery of my every step. I couldn't imagine any mice with all these loud women, yet I couldn't be too careful. I quickly showered, but decided not to call Don that night. I was depressed and didn't want to feel dejected on Thanksgiving night.

As I climbed up on my safe space, I could see a woman directly across the aisle from me had a small television on. I later learned you could buy a TV from commissary if you had enough money, or a family member could send one in to you. That counted me out.

The woman, and several of those around her, was watching the 1996 Arnold Schwarzenegger Christmas film *Jingle All the Way.* I grabbed my pillow and turned to lie facing the foot of the bed so I could see the movie as well. Although saddened I wasn't home watching it from my own comfy couch with Don and Jen; I was comforted by the fact that I was able to enjoy this small indulgence. I actually found myself occasionally laughing and enjoying this time. It felt good to be able to take my mind off of things for a short while.

As I returned to the head of the bed for lights out that night, I softly prayed *"Thank you God. Thank you for showers and TV's today."* Every day was another day of realizing that for some reason God was in fact "preserving" me. But for what purpose? There had been so many times in my life of which I had felt threatened, beaten down, and helpless. I had blamed God for these things in my life; often times vowing to never trust or believe in anyone or anything again.

Black Friday

"⁴ I will stretch out my hand against Judah and against all who live in Jerusalem . . ⁶ those who turn back from following the LORD and neither seek the LORD nor inquire of him. . .. ¹⁵ That day will be a day of wrath . . . a day of darkness and gloom, a day of clouds and blackness . . . ¹⁸ Neither their silver nor their gold will be able to save them on the day of the LORD's wrath."
Zephaniah 1: 4-18

I had never really grasped the whole concept of Black Friday. I mean I understood it was the day after Thanksgiving, and was regarded as the first day of the traditional Christmas shopping season. But just as in the movie I had watched the night before, I had heard so many senseless stories of people staking out their places in long lines hours before the doors opened at 6:00am; fighting each other for greatly reduced items; as well as the outright brawls, serious injuries and even deaths that had been attributed to this day.

I had a very good friend who once told me horror stories of when she and her sister would go shopping on this day every year. One year they were right in there with everyone fighting over a Cabbage Patch doll for her daughter. I was appalled as they both laughed and told the story of how they had yelled, cursed and scratched people to get to this doll. At the time I remember thinking I couldn't even imagine being so materialistic and ridiculous as actually fighting people for something for a 3-year-old!

But then again, I couldn't make sense of my own life, or the crazy decisions I had made either. Was I not even more ridiculous or materialistic to think I could lie, steal and cheat my way to try to hang on to something I thought to be so valuable? And to what end did it accomplish? Nothing at all. I had lost everything: my home, my vehicle, my job, my family, my dignity and my freedom.

And yet, I was learning that God had not turned His back on me. He was slowly, but consistently teaching me of His ways. He was instilling within me what true love, grace forgiveness, and restoration really was. I didn't understand this God of mercy and redemption. Once again, I asked myself what could possibly be the reason? He had saved me from suicide. He had protected me from Peaches. He brought me through so many other unspeakable events in my life. Could He in fact be "preserving" me for something I could not possibly understand or comprehend at this time?

"I will never forget your precepts, for by them you have preserved my life."

Psalm 119:93

40 Days and 40 Nights

"And rain fell on the earth forty days and forty nights."
*Genesis 7:12 (**Noah**)*

"Then Moses entered the cloud as he went on up the mountain. And he stayed on the mountain forty days and forty nights."
*Exodus 24:18 (**Moses**)*

"And he arose and ate and drank, and went in the strength of that food forty day and forty nights to Horeb, the mount of God."
*1 Kings 19:8 (**Elijah**)*

". . . and he was in the wilderness forty days, being tempted by Satan. He was with the wild animals, and angels attended him."
*Mark 1:134 (**Jesus**)*

"After his suffering, he presented himself to them and gave many convincing proofs that he was alive. He appeared to them over a period of forty days and spoke about the kingdom of God."
*Acts 1:3 (**Jesus**)*

Mail and commissary orders were distributed around 8:00am that morning. I thought surely it must be Christmas morning. I was overjoyed with my lavish cocoanut-scented body wash, tropical fruit-smelling shampoo, Suave deodorant, blue plastic razor and a Snicker's bar! Red was still at work. I would have to tell her of my treasures later that day.

I hadn't received any mail that morning; but maybe right now that was a good thing. The few letters I had received from my mom had been so discouraging and hurtful. I couldn't understand why my parents had appeared to be so supportive in the beginning; but were now cold and insensitive to me. They told me how selfish I was, and I was not a good parent to allow Jennifer to stay at the apartment. I had also been painstakingly awaiting each day for letters, a card, or some other form of communication from Don. But other than the $20 he had originally asked Mom to put on my books, he never sent anything else at all.

Bless their hearts, all my daughters had been writing to me; trying to encourage me by telling me what was going on with everyone, and that they loved and missed me. I don't know what I would have done without them. I also knew my son, Jamie, was thinking of me, and his heart was broken for me, as well. The girls told me he was really taking it hard.

I realized the excruciating strain I had caused for everyone; but as much as I had hurt them, I needed to look deep within myself and focus on myself right now. I needed to learn how to stop hating myself so much. I needed to heal. I needed to believe that somehow, I could come through this and try to start all over again. I needed hope - and I needed Jesus. But I didn't know how to truly find Him. I was still searching for that relationship.

After indulging in my commissary items, I decided to read a little. After several minutes, an inmate I had never met before stopped at my bunk. A short, older, rather plump lady, she inquired "Hey. I'm Nora. I noticed you reading the Bible. What's your name?"

I sat up and took in all the features of this very pleasant, Grandmotherly black woman; with almost all-white hair, braided in nice even rows on top of her head. Missing several of her teeth, she smiled from ear to ear.

I answered her "Nanette. Yeah, I've been reading this, trying to figure out a lot of things right now."

"What is it you don't understand? Maybe I can help you," she continued. She assured me she was very knowledgeable of the Bible. Not quite sure that I wanted to trust this woman, yet how could I not . . . with her calm and warm demeanor? I slid down off the bunk and we walked to the common area to talk.

The Price is Right was viewing on the television on the wall, but surprisingly, I really wasn't distracted by it. Nora did seem to know a lot of things about the Bible, and rattled off numerous verses and stories she had read. I listened intently of her explanations and accounts of several of the more *"well-known"* Bible figures, but most especially about Jesus.

Eventually it became quite noisy in the general gathering area; so, we signed out, put on our heavy coats, and walked to the chapel. We were surprised the doors were unlocked and we were able to get inside the building. A rather small church, we walked down the center aisle, and sat in the pews near the front of the chapel. There was a very large wooden cross on the back wall of the vestibule area, with a podium and about twelve chairs arranged to the right side. I assumed that area must be for the choir. I welcomed this sacred and serene atmosphere. It was definitely a sanctuary - a place of preservation, peace and protection.

As we continued our discussion, I proceeded to tell Nora about my family life growing up - my children, grandchildren, and recent life before coming to prison. When I explained to her all of the turmoil of the last several weeks, my extended time in Admissions, and all the fear I had endured, she asked "How long you been down for?"

I had methodically crossed off each day from my small laminated calendar, as well as the daily devotionals I would read each morning; so, I didn't hesitate when I responded "Today is 40 days."

She instantly stopped me. "Do you understand the significance of 40 days?" she asked.

Puzzled, I answered "No." She opened up her Bible and read several different verses regarding the many instances of God's instructions, days of trial, or waiting periods regarding Noah, Moses, Elijah, Jonah, and Jesus.

"Do you understand that 40 days represents the temptation, probation, judgement and hardship before an answer or sign is given that God has intervened? At the end of the testing comes a time or item of blessing; a time to be spared of any more suffering or pain. You have been blessed."

I instantly felt goose bumps all up and down my arms, and butterflies in my stomach. I almost felt sick to my stomach. I felt that she must be an angel sent to tell me these things; to comfort me, to encourage me, to let me know that God was very real. God had indeed blessed me to protect and bring me out of that dangerous situation. He had provided me with several new freedoms within the compound; as well as phone calls, showers, televisions and small tokens of His love with my commissary items - things I normally would have never been appreciative of.

We walked back to the dorm as it was getting close to lunchtime. I knew that Red was probably wondering where I had been. When we reached my bunk, I hugged Nora, thanked her, and told her we would meet again soon. Excited to tell Red of my new friend and of all that she had told me, I climbed up on the bed, only to see that she was covered up in her blanket. I just let her sleep. We would talk after lunch.

Cards, Friendship & Letters from Home

I didn't work with Red that night for the dinner shift as Amnesty had invited me to play cards with her and some of the other women. "You play cards?" she had asked me earlier.

"Yea, a little. What kind?" I inquired.

"What do you know how to play?" she continued.

"Hearts, Euchre, and a little Poker." I explained further that although it had been many years ago; my ex-husband and I used to play cards almost every week-end with our friends.

"That's a start. At least you know the basics and will pick up on the game," she urged me. I felt encouraged that others had included me to join them.

I actually looked forward to playing cards on a Friday night. I knew it would help take my mind of off things at home right now. As much as I wanted to call the apartment, I knew no one would be there to answer. Friday nights were when Don and I would go out to eat and stop at the local VFW hall afterwards for drinks. I knew for certain he would still go out with his friends to the bar. Friday nights were also when Jennifer would cheer at the high school football games. I knew she would be with her friends at the game. I wanted them to continue to go out and have fun, but it was so hard not being there with them.

I also hated to let Red down. I promised her it would just be for this one night. She assured me it was okay. "Besides, you're not getting paid to help me. You're just keeping me company. Have a good time!" I was so grateful of her friendship.

I did have a good time. It was fun to be able to laugh a little bit again. Someone made popcorn and someone else brought soda pop they had purchased from commissary. A couple other women made fudge out of marshmallows & chocolate bars they cooked in the microwave. "Here, try a piece of this. This

117

stuff is the bomb!" one of the ladies making the fudge offered me. Understanding that most of the women were not willing, or able to share what little bit they did have available to them; I was very grateful for the small bowl of popcorn and a bite of the fudge that was extended to me.

I was happy that night. I felt safe and secure in this new setting. This had not been a Black Friday for me at all - it had been a very Good Friday.

Exhausted from all the adventures of the day, I once again made my way to the top of the bunk where I lay quietly thinking of my kids and Don. I would do anything to only see them, hold them; and tell them how sorry I was, and how much I loved them. I was tremendously homesick, but knew I needed to get my life together first.

"Thank you for this day God. You have blessed me and brought me through this time of fear and worry. I know there is still so much I have yet to face, but somehow, I'll make it. Just don't leave me God. Don't ever leave me. And please, please take care of Jennifer and my kids and grandsons." I don't recall what else may have been on my mind. I silently and peacefully fell asleep.

Early Saturday morning was a "sleeping" count. I was especially pleased we didn't have to get up at 5:00am, get dressed, clean the area around us, make the beds, or stand at the foot of our bunks for count. Lights were left off and the CO's conducted count while we stayed in bed. I am not usually an early morning person or a breakfast eater, so I was very content to just stay in bed and sleep all morning. Lunch would be here soon enough.

Mail was distributed later that morning, about 10:00am. I was surprised to hear my name called. I awkwardly slid down off the bed long enough to pick up my mail. Although I had just spoken with Don a few days earlier, I was still hopeful that maybe I would receive a letter of encouragement, or possibly a card telling me he still loved me. I just didn't want to hear any bad news - I couldn't take it right now.

When the CO handed me the envelope, my anxiety level was eased to see it was from Jennifer. I quickly climbed up on my bed and opened the letter:

(No date) *"Dear Mom, I just got your letters. I hope you are doing ok. I know you say you are, but I know you're not, and Mom quit worrying about me. I'm fine, I just miss you and just keep thinking about you being in there is the only thing that makes me sad. I just wish I could do something and I hate it because I can't. I just don't want you to be sad. If I could switch you places I would in a heartbeat. I just don't want you to be in there on Christmas, you don't deserve it. You deserve to be here with your family and the only thing I want for Christmas is for you to be happy since I know you can't come home. You will be home soon, and everything will be back the way it used to be except better. I hope Don don't think I want to go live with Dad right now, because I don't. I haven't even thought about it. I am going to wait right here till you get out and I would <u>never</u> give up on you Mom. You just made a mistake and I couldn't have asked for a better Mom than you because you will do anything to make us happy, and I know I have said some things in the past but I really didn't mean any of them, and you will never hear them come out of my mouth again. I look up to you Mom because you can do anything that you want to do, and you are always thinking about others before yourself and that's why I love you so much. But no, I don't want to go live with Dad right now. I want to finish school and I'm happy here, and Don is really great. I don't know what would have happened if you would have never met him. I got my (school) pictures back but they are ugly. I hope I get a job then I can kinda help Don out. Dad is taking me to get my license over Christmas break, hopefully. But I don't have a car anyways. But oh well. Write me back soon. I miss you! Much Love, Jenny"*

Nanette T. Friend

As I sat with tears running down my face, I felt somewhat encouraged again. *"Thank you, God. Thank you so much for my amazing kids and Jennifer; bless her heart."* I needed to hear that - and from my 16-year old daughter, was incredible. I had been so afraid she was still mad at me and would never forgive me. I couldn't blame her if she didn't. I never knew how very blessed and proud I was of my children - *ALL* of them, until now. Often times it takes a crisis for families to come together; and they certainly did that for me.

"Children are a heritage from the LORD, offspring a reward from Him."

Psalm 127:3

Answered Prayers

Grateful the dining area was not very far from the dorm as cold winds were once again whipping at our faces, Red and I quickly walked back to the dorm after lunch. We decided to read and write letters that afternoon. I answered Jen and thanked her for her letter, and told her I how much I had needed to hear her words. I asked how Don was doing as I hadn't heard from him, and he appeared to be so depressed. I explained that I was hoping to be allowed to go to the Pre-Release Center so I could be much closer to home, and to have them come to visit me there. I also told her how much I missed everyone and was so homesick. I finished my letter and put it under my pillow until I could stop at the mailbox before dinner that night.

Sunday was another lazy morning to sleep in; however, I was anxious to go to church services with Nora later that day.

After the service we walked back to the dorm and continued our conversation until we reached my bunk.

"I guess I need to be gettin' me some rest now" Nora stated as she headed down the corridor toward her area. Then she stopped and turned back, and as an afterthought, "You think I could get your phone number? I mean, you know if you might be leaving here soon, then we can stay in contact when we get back out on the streets." I wasn't quite sure that I would really be staying in contact with anyone other than Red, but I didn't think it would hurt anything. So, I agreed to give her my phone number.

Monday afternoon I asked Red "I keep wondering why I haven't been assigned to any meetings or work detail yet. You think it's because this is just a temporary location for me? Do you think it could mean I have a chance to go to the Pre-Release Center?"

"I dunno" she answered. "You know they don't tell you nothin' until the very minute you are leaving or need to be someplace."

"Yeah, but I guess I think it's been crazy no one has said anything at all about any assignments. It's like I just keep hangin' out with nothing to do. I mean, I'm really not complaining . . . just wondering."

"Well, you'll know soon enough by tomorrow morning 'cause anyone going out will get an early morning wakeup call. So have your things ready just in case," she explained.

"Ok I will. If so, I'm sure gonna miss you, Red. Please stay in contact with me. I'll write to you and see what's going on with you. I know you don't have much more time before you go back to Cincinnati."

"I will. I promise," she said. I didn't know it then, but that would be the last time I would ever see or hear from Red again. I wrote her a couple of times after I left Maryswood, but never received a response. I do think of her often. I know that she was the friend and angel God sent to watch over me during my time at the prison.

It was 4:00am Tuesday morning. The bright light of the flashlight shining in my eyes, the CO quietly tried to wake me up. "Come on Friend. Let's go. You're transporting out today. Get your things and meet me at the front desk."

I had been in a deep, restful sleep; but quickly awoke and scrambled to get my thoughts, and my things together. After I had dressed and gathered everything up in a bag, I reached over the top of the wall and whispered "Red, Red. I'm leaving. Can you hear me? I'm going out today."

She raised up and turned around to face me. "Ok, be careful. Miss you girl," she whispered.

"Miss you too. I'll write soon." I scrambled down from the bunk and headed for the atrium area. My heart was beating rapidly at the excitement of knowing that I was finally leaving this awful compound forever. I was so relieved to know I wouldn't have to keep looking over my shoulder to see if anyone was going to attack me. *"Oh, thank you God! Thank you, thank you! I can't believe I am finally leaving here!"*

As we stepped out into the bitter cold, dark morning, the CO walked me to the discharge building. Joined there by six or seven other women, we were soon escorted down a set of dark, steep cellar steps. Cold, damp and musty-smelling, and filled with spider webs; it reminded me of the scary, outside cellarway of my Nana and Papa's old home.

As we entered the room, I thought we certainly must be in the midst of a horror movie. It was literally an old dark, damp basement, with a single bright light-bulb hanging from the center of the ceiling. We stepped onto a huge piece of dark green carpet that was just lying atop the dirt floor. The walls were constructed of old bricks, and lined with wooden shelves filled with bright orange jumpsuits of every size. There were also rows of ankle chains and hand-cuffs hanging from large hooks on the walls. It was almost as if this could be a torture chamber of sorts. I was grateful to be able to leave, but I sure wanted to get out of that dungeon as soon as possible!

The COs assigned to us that morning instructed us to leave our bags of belongings on a long table against the wall for inspection; and then "Line up!" After roll call, we were told to select a jumpsuit that would fit and return to our place in line. "Listen up! Face forward at *all* times, *everything* off, and wait until everyone has been fully inspected. If we find that you are hiding or attempting to transfer anything out with you, you will *not* be leaving here today!"

Humiliating once again, the strip search began with full and complete body and cavity check. As demeaning and embarrassing as it was, I knew every woman there was suffering through the same horrific ordeal. It was appalling enough, but then to stand there stark naked in that cold and creepy room, was excruciating to say the least.

Once the full search was completed, we were instructed to dress in our now bright-orange jumpsuits and prepare to be shackled. Now clad in warm coats and shoes, chains were first placed about our wrists. Then ankles bracelets were secured with just enough space between them to be able to climb the steps of the cellar, and onto the awaiting bus. A CO stationed at the door of the van helped us step up into the vehicle.

One by one we slowly made our way to our seats. A thin glaze of ice still upon the window panes, I could see my breath in the cold air. The driver assured us it would be warming up soon enough. I gazed out into the dark cold morning, and remember thanking God with all my heart that I was finally moving out of the compound and to a safer facility. I never, ever wanted to see this place again. As the bus slowly pulled away and through the huge entrance gates, every sense of fear and worry left my heart and soul. I realized I would still be imprisoned, but the Pre-Release Center sounded to be an entirely different atmosphere; and so much closer to home for me. I felt a huge sense of relief and gratitude to be offered this option to serve the rest of my time.

I sat quietly in my seat, not speaking to anyone. Actually, no one was talking. I think we were all too cold and too tired to talk. Shivering and attempting to keep my hands warm, I kept rubbing them together; never realizing that with every move I made, the shackles were tightening up about my wrist. But right now, that was the least of my worries. I didn't care about the discomfort. I could only pray, thanking God again for His answered prayer.

*"Oh, and God? If we do get to have our own rooms with roommates, could I **please** have someone who doesn't swear all the time and who reads the Bible?"* I guess I thought that would ensure I would be in a much safer place with others.

"You will be secure, because there is hope; you will look about you and take your rest in safety. You will lie down, with no one to make you afraid, and many will court your favor."

Job11:18-19

CHAPTER 8

❧ *Conclusion* ❧

n: A reasoned judgment; the last part of something; result or outcome; trial of strength or skill; a final summation; the final decision or the final part; an act or instance of concluding.

A Reasoned Judgement

"Therefore, say to the Israelites: 'I am the LORD, and I will bring you out from under the yoke of the Egyptians. I will free you from being slaves to them, and I will redeem you with an outstretched arm and with mighty acts of judgment."

Exodus 6:6

Concluding seven long weeks confined within the concrete walls and barbed wire of Maryswood, I was truly grateful to be leaving this place of perceived fear and terror. I no longer felt that never-ending threat of Peaches' last words to me: *". . . you think you got away from me? I know right where you are!"* With well over an hour to travel, at long-last I was now on the bus on my way to the Pre-Release Center to serve the remainder of my year-long sentence.

However, as I continued to stare out the icy glass window of the bus, I knew there would be no way to know what I might be facing in this new institutional environment. There could very possibly be yet another "Peaches" upon this compound, as well. Although I did understand that some of the specifications were the following: 1) You must have less than two years left to serve; 2) You were being "prepared" to be released back into society; and 3) This was a minimum-security facility - I couldn't imagine anyone that close to going home would do anything to jeopardize their situation. I could only pray for safety and protection.

And yet I was leaving there seeking and somewhat accepting of something way beyond my ability to comprehend within the "tangible" world I had been living in. I was anxious to learn, to understand and find this new-found hope. I knew if I could see it, touch it, hear or smell it, I believed it to be true. In the back of my mind, I always believed there was a God; only that He didn't exist for *me*. However, this new "feeling" or "impression" that now resided deep within my soul was something I could not ignore; nor truly understand, or possibly conceive to be as "truth" . . . yet.

Trial of Strength or Skill

"You saw with your own eyes the great trials, the signs and wonders, the mighty hand and outstretched arm, with which the LORD your God brought you out."

Deut 7:19

There was no doubt in my mind that God was with me. There were too many things that had taken place that were not something I could "logically" explain. I didn't know it then, but God was genuinely teaching me about "truth" - of who He was, and of the plans He had for me. But He needed me to accept the truth of who I was, what I was capable of, and what He wanted for me first. These were all things I could not comprehend at the time.

Understanding and accepting my fate as a criminal was one thing. But to accept and understand that never-ending pain deep within my heart as a failure in the eyes of everyone else, was something I couldn't grasp. My shame, embarrassment, and total humiliation as a person, as a mother, as a daughter or sister, was devastating within itself. I just couldn't accept the truth of who I had become, or forgive myself of the horrible things I had done. However, you don't typically learn your true feelings and deepest desires just because you want to; they are revealed once you've faced the truths you tend to hide from. Especially if you push the limits like I did for so long, you may sometimes have to soak in your pain for a while before God retrieves you. Thankfully, He really does only allow as much struggle as is necessary to bring us to the place of surrender, the place of peace and clarity that we most long for.

The Secret Things of God ~ Defining: Truth

n: Sincerity in action, character, and utterance; the state of being the case; the body of real things, events, and facts; a transcendent fundamental or spiritual reality; a judgment, proposition, or idea that is true or accepted as true; the body of true statements and propositions.

Simple, or *"relative"* truth tells us that Sacramento is the Capitol of California; ice cream is a sweet and delicious treat; flowers are beautiful and smell delightful, and in the United States, all drivers must drive an automobile on the right side of the road. We accept all of these things as being true because we can see, taste, smell or prove these things to be a "fact", and therefore accepted as truth.

Other "truths" are left up to us to determine to be true or false. God created us to have "free will" and character; to make decisions that may determine what is best for us to live a happy and productive life, as well as to decide what should become of us once we depart from this earthly life. Without free will, all decisions would not be genuine. As in any relationship, if God *made*, or caused us to believe a certain way, perform certain tasks or rituals, love Him because He forced us to do so; then there is no "truth" of our character, our virtue, or our true love for Him.

"2 The woman said to the serpent, "We may eat fruit from the trees in the garden, 3 but God did say, 'You must not eat fruit from the tree that is in the middle of the garden, and you must not touch it, or you will die'." 4 "You will not certainly die," the serpent said to the woman. 5 "For God knows that when you eat from it your eyes will be opened, and you will be like God, knowing good and evil."

Genesis 2-5

From the very beginning of Creation of Adam and Eve, the divine hope of purity and innocence was lost within lies and deception. Satan, disguised as a serpent, appeared to Eve and told her an out and out blatant lie; deceiving her into thinking that God only had unworthy motives for her and her husband. The statement was only half true. Their eyes *would* be open to good and evil for sure, but the result would be quite different from what the serpent had promised. Originally created and only meant to know what good, love, beauty and pleasure would be, now the couple would understand that evil, sin and unrighteousness existed, and be forced to live in a world filled with both.

God never intended for man to have to bear the burden of having to decide between good and evil, right and wrong. But having graciously given man the power of free will and decision making, the fall of man was swift and immediate. Sacrifice would now have to be required as a part of worship; as well as to seek and receive the forgiveness of sin.

As newborn infants, we are immediately exposed to a society based upon sin, deceit, untruthfulness and defamation. Although man is taught society's virtues of good and evil, truth and deception, as well as love and hate, the human race is destined to be born with an evil and sinful nature.

How many times when we feel that life is good, safe, or valuable, we don't *feel* the need to seek out God? We've got this. We are in control, and don't require any additional "help" or grace from God. We find our security in other people, relationships, money or careers. Or possibly we try to replace the pain in our life with the temporary relief of alcohol, drugs, gambling or sex. Often times, in the weakness of the human race, we have to endure many trials, pain or loss before we finally do seek God. But when faced with devastation from lost relationships or the death of a loved one; pain that is inflicted upon us either emotionally or physically; loss of jobs, security, homes, or our children; when we have hit rock bottom and find ourselves in a situation that we know of no way out - do we then, and ONLY then reach out to God?

We pray, beg, and make deals with Him. If *ONLY* He will help us this one time, provide us with all that we need, get us out of debt, jail or physical pain; bring back the love of our life, or take away the excruciating pain of the death of someone we have cherished. Only then do we promise we will give our life to Him and assure Him we will do whatever He asks of us. How many times I had made this promise to God, over and over again. Of course, I never went so far as to say I would actually *go* to church or to give my life to Him; only that I would *help* Him ~ you know, like giving to the poor - as IF God needed my help!

Triumph over trial

"Then you will know the truth, and the truth will set you free."
John 8:32

Human nature is to run with the answer we can explain, to go with the loud voice of consensus versus the lone whisper within; and to speed ahead with the solution that makes sense to our minds, our training, our background and experience (in other words, our own "understanding"). This is a very profound truth, but it is also essential to ultimately discerning what God wants you to do.

When you find yourself scared, alone, confused and hurting; you desire, you *yearn* for comfort, peace, love and understanding. *That* yearning is your true desire - and God's delight. That's what you want to lock into and figure out. And that's exactly what God wants to show you, and reward you with if you will be patient and let Him do what He does best.

I still didn't understand it at the time, but God was desperately trying to show me, teach me the **truth** - about the saving grace of Jesus Christ and the loving Spirit that could live deep within my heart. For only He knows that when our heart's desires are met, we are truly satisfied, and the contentment lasts. God knew that for me, the only way I could ever be accepting of Him and His great love for me, was to bring me to my knees, to experience the trials, the pain and the eventual surrender.

Eventually, I had to have to face the truth - and oftentimes the truth hurts - a *lot*. Most times, we are not willing or prepared to do all it requires to admit the truth. Through everything I *anticipated* to be true, through understating the *creation* of who I was, *realizing* the *condition* of my heart, accepting the *conviction* of my soul, and *determined* to *preserve* all that God had for me - was I finally able to acknowledge the truth of who He was within me.

A Final Summation; God's Story Never Ends

"The man who saw it has given testimony, and his testimony is true. He knows that he tells the truth, and he testifies so that you also may believe."

John 19:35

For many years, my true desire has been to shout from the mountain tops, and proclaim the undeniable authenticity of God, and who He is. But in doing so, I knew I would have to reveal the unspeakable truth, and sometimes unbearable sins of my own life. Otherwise, how could I possibly make known the miracles, visions, life changing moments, hope, and understanding of who God has been in my life; without bearing the reality of the facts leading up to His presence in my heart?

Please understand this is most definitely not the *conclusion* of my (entire) story - by any means at all. This is simply the "closing" of the *first part* of this very long journey - my continued search for some form of sanity, understanding, and *truth* in my life. It wouldn't be until my actual incarceration at the Pre-Release Center, that I would learn and accept the truth of Jesus Christ. Once again, I knew He existed; but I did not understand His role in my heart, my soul or my life. I did not understand or know of the great love He had for me, or of the gifts He so graciously wanted to give to me.

There are countless more stories, experiences, miracles and lessons God was taking me through for this one book alone. He had captured my attention. He was occupying the awareness in my mind, and the empty place in my heart.

I was so lost, but I didn't know *how* to change. I didn't know where to begin. I truly didn't believe there was any *truth* for me. My whole life had been a series of lies, confusion, deceit and condemnation. How do you know what to look for when you have never experienced what *truth* is?

If you find yourself broken, hurt, desperate, sick, confused, or imprisoned, and have no place to turn - possibly you have lost your home, your children, your spouse, or any hope for your future. Your life may be filled with constant worry, depression and fear. You or your loved ones may suffer from overwhelming financial burdens, addictions, serious mental or physical illness, captivity or imprisonment; or other serious life-changing afflictions. How do you possibly break free from these chains of bondage and oppression?

Please join me as I reveal God's story of my on-going journey with Him into the next book of this series, entitled **Defining Faith.** I will take you through my incarceration at the pre-release center, where you will meet Sofie, Cricket, Tanisha and Angel. It was here, in the midst of yet more shake-downs, let-downs, break-ups, heart-aches, hurdles and countless blessings: that I finally begin to realize the precious gift He was unfolding for me. Filled with miracles, visions and revelations, follow me as I share with you the *amazing grace* and redemption . . . that saved a wretch like me.

"However, as it is written: 'What no eye has seen, what no ear has heard, and what no human mind has conceived' the things God has prepared for those who love him . . ."

1 Corinthians 2:9

❧ ACKNOWLEDGEMENTS ❧

n. The act of acknowledging or state of being acknowledged. Something done or given as an expression of thanks or appreciation, as a reply to a message, etc. Recognition of existence or truth of something.

For the hours spent in prayer, fasting, typing, deadlines, tears, struggle deep within my heart, editing, searching for truth and kindness, encouragement, love, and great patience, I wish to thank and acknowledge:

* My Father God, most precious Jesus Christ and Savior, and wonderful Holy Spirit of whom provided me the dream, passion, determination and drive to keep writing - to share HIS "truth".

* My four loving and remarkable children:

Frank James (Jamie), Jodi Kathleen, Jillian Joyce, and Jennifer Lynne -

and their spouses: Danielle, Jason (I.), Jason (P.), and Jon

My amazing and precious grandchildren - All 14 of them: Dusty (Danielle), Danny (Kendra), Christopher (Emily), Jacob (Josh), Ethan, Dylan, Cole, Kaylynn Nanette and Great-grandchildren: Joshua, Dustin Scott, Isabella (Bella), Lyla Joy, Leonard James and Danilynn Dawn.

I love and cherish each and every one of you. You are my life and my heart. Thank you for continuing to love and encourage me throughout my trials and tribulation, and eventually the many joys of my life.

* To my husband and the love of my life, Daniel (Danny) Miller. God sent you to me at a time in my life when I was fighting the demons of loneliness and a lack of companionship. You allowed me to be able to love again, to open my heart and

mind to the true values of who God created us to be . . . man and wife together. You have encouraged me and given me my "space" to finish this first part of the journey.

My Mother and extended family of whom I truly seek love and understanding.

* *Chaplain Scott Hayes* . . . whose testimony of his own "demons", sins, conviction and prison time gave me the courage and insight to come forward. . . who has consistently and undeniably provided the encouragement, confirmation, conviction, truth, and the Word of Jesus Christ to inmates and families everywhere.

Mrs. Connie Cameron, Author, Columnist, Inspirational Speaker, and loving friend; as well as confidant, mentor and counselor. I love you dearly my sister in Christ.

* *Ms. Patricia Collins,* Women's Chaplain, mentor, prayer warrior and wonderful friend. Thank you for your continued encouragement and prayers.

* *Ms. Heather McWilliams,* amazing friend, sounding board, advisor and technical support. Thank you for the hours you have put in to help me with "social media" and internet education. I would truly be lost without you.

* *Ms. Angie Roffey,* my one true "success story." You have never given up the struggle and have continued to search with all of your heart God's great purpose for your life. Thank you for your never-ending "feed-back," love, support and friendship, dear heart.

*And finally, but most certainly not least, I am in forever debt to my faithful editor, *Mr. Scott Wilson.* You have served as my counselor, advisor, and most valued friend. Your constant support, validation and firm reinforcement have provided me with the guidance, encouragement and will to stay focused through every last word. I cannot begin to thank you enough for your dedication and commitment to this long journey we have traveled together. I am hopeful one day I am indeed able to thank you with that membership to the Country Club golf course.

**To My Victims* ~ a sincere apology. I have longed to someday and publicly tell you how truly sorry I am for the horrible crime I have committed against you. It has been a long road that I have struggled with every piece of torment, shame and humiliation within me. I could never quite understand that you were always so very kind and tolerant of me. Please know that I sincerely pray to someday be able to restore a very large part of the debt that I owe you. Not only in finances, but in some form of retribution (justice) of my sins and actions against you. I am hopeful that by coming forward and telling the truth, I will be able to start that healing process for all of you. I will begin by asking you to please forgive me.

Printed in the United States
By Bookmasters